A Christmas Companion

Recipes, Traditions and Customs from Around the World

BY

JIM CHARLTON & MARIA ROBBINS

A Perigee Book

Perigee Books
are published by
The Putnam Publishing Group
200 Madison Avenue
New York, NY 10016

Published simultaneously in Canada

Designed by Hudson Studio

Library of Congress Cataloging in Publication Data

A Christmas Companion recipes, traditions, and customs from
around the world/ by Jim Charlton and Maria Robbins
p. cm.
Includes index.
ISBN 0-399-51564-X
1. Christmas cookery. 2. Christmas decorations. 3. Christmas.
I. Charlton, James, 1939– . II. Title.
TX739.2.C45P65 1989 89-15935 CIP
641.5'66—dc20

Printed in the United States of America
1 2 3 4 5 6 7 8 9 10

TABLE OF CONTENTS

A CHRISTMAS COMPANION

Christmas Before Christmas

It has been said that Christmas, in addition to its religious significance as the celebration of the birth of Jesus, has become the focus of a worldwide state of mind—the universal human need for hope, warmth, and good cheer, especially in those dreary winter months when not only the sun but the human spirit itself is often at a low ebb.

There is actually no evidence that the historical Jesus was born in December. His birth was not celebrated then until nearly four hundred years after his death, and the term "Christ's Mass" wasn't used until the eleventh century.

But long before the birth of Christ, the 25th of December was the date of the Roman winter solstice, the midpoint of a festive season that extended from the Saturnalia, which began on December 17, and was a festival of tribute to Saturn, the god of plenty, to the Kalends in January, which marked the beginning of the New Year. At the same time of year the Teutons in the north celebrated the festival of Yule, and the Mithraic religion of Persia, an early competitor of Christianity, celebrated the birth of the unconquered sun. In the Jewish tradition midwinter was the occasion for the annual cleansing of the Temple, a very important holiday. The central theme of all these festivals, the rebirth of hope, was also central to the gospel of Jesus, and as Christianity gained acceptance among the people of Europe, it was completely natural that older customs and newer beliefs should blend together—the new religion sometimes simply adopting the practices of the old ones, sometimes adapting parts of them to serve a new belief.

The burning of the Yule log, for instance, harks back to a Norse tradition of burning oak logs in honor of Thor. It also reflects the Celtic belief in the sacredness of perpetual fire—this year's log is lighted with a brand from the log of the year before.

So it should not be surprising if in celebrating Christmas we find ourselves perpetuating customs and beliefs that can be traced back to the very earliest rituals of mankind. When we decorate our tree, exchange our gifts, drink our wassail, sit down to our feast, or kiss under the mistletoe, we are not merely observing a particular religious holiday, but honoring all the ancient and enduring hopes and fears of mankind.

Christmas in the British Isles

The modern ideal of Christmas, especially in the United States and Great Britain, stems more or less directly from the English Victorian Christmas, as heartwarmingly and romantically captured by Charles Dickens. Santa Claus is known as Father Christmas in Britain, and the gifts he brings are opened on Christmas afternoon. Letters addressed to him detailing the specific nature of hoped-for presents are tossed in the fireplace rather than actually posted. Requests are thought more likely to be granted if the draft carries the letter up the chimney.

The British have a tale to explain the custom of hanging stockings from the mantelpiece. It seems that Father Christmas once dropped some gold coins while coming down a chimney. They would have fallen through the ash grate and been lost had they not landed in a stocking that had been hung up to dry. Since that time stockings have been hung at the hearth.

In England the roasted boar's head has long been associated with Christmas feasting and before that with the Norse custom of sacrificing a boar at Yuletide in honor of the god Freyr. It is said that a student at Oxford's Queen's College, empty-handed except for his copy of Aristotle, was attacked on Christmas Day by a wild boar. At a loss for a weapon with which to defend himself, he choked the beast by shoving the book down its throat. Wanting only to have his copy of Aristotle back, the student cut off the head of the boar and brought it back to the college, where, at the high table, the first boar's head feast was celebrated, even as it is with much pomp and ritual to this day.

The custom of "wassailing" has no direct religious significance, but it reflects all the warm indulgent toasting and merriment associated with the season. The word is derived from the Anglo-Saxon phrase *waes hael*, meaning "good health." Originally, wassail was a beverage made of mulled ale, eggs, curdled cream, roasted apples, nuts, and spices.

Wassail, wassail, all over the town
Our bread it is white and our ale it is brown;
Our bowl it is made of the green maple tree,
In the wassail bowl we'll drink unto thee.

Traditional English song

The custom of serving wassail supposedly began when a Saxon maiden of renowned beauty named Rowena presented to Prince Vortigen a bowl of wine and toasted him by saying, "Waes hael." Over the centuries a great deal of ceremony has evolved around the custom of wassail drinking, with much attention paid to the carrying in of the great bowl, the singing of a traditional carol in praise of the drink, and finally to the tasting of the mixture itself, which is customarily served steaming hot.

In the massive hearths of the great halls of feudal England it was the custom on Christmas Eve to burn a special Yule log. The arrival of the log was an occasion for celebration and singing, and the log itself was chosen with ritual care and was always huge—it was expected to burn until Epiphany, on January 6. Fragments of the spent log were always saved carefully to light the Yule fire the following year.

In fifteenth-century England there was a revival of some of the older midwinter customs, including many that could be traced back to the Saturnalian revels of ancient Rome. One such custom had to do with the master of the revels, who became known as the Lord of Misrule, and reigned over an upside-down world where servants were waited upon by their masters, and even the king had to learn how to be humble (for one day, in any case).

Christmas at the Tudor Court of Henry VIII

At Christmas the pillars in the gardens were decorated with pearls, artificial flowers of silk and gold, pomegranates and roses; the peacock was roasted, sewn into its plumage, covered with leaf gold, stuffed with spices and sweet herbs and gilded with egg yolk.

Consuming Passions,
Philippa Pullar

At Christmastime in the Cotswolds, in Hampshire, and in other areas of England, masked players called mummers (because, like mimes, they do not speak) still parade and sing, wearing grotesque costumes and performing ancient and often rowdy pantomimes and tableaux that relate to the basic themes of death and resurrection. Though discouraged by the Church, mumming still survives as a Christmas tradition in some areas of England. In the U.S. there is a mummers parade in Philadelphia on New Year's Day.

The hanging of holly and other greens at Christmastime is a British tradition whose source goes back so far in history as to be virtually lost. Certainly it can be said that the greenery, with its promise of spring, helps lift any spirits that may be sagging under the weight of winter's gloom. And the tradition of kissing under a sprig of mistletoe, descended from ancient Druid rites and thus authentically early British, no doubt brings a measure of joy wherever it is followed.

The practice of singing songs appropriate to the Christmas season, either as an adjunct to church services or when sung by a strolling band of serenaders, is also very English. Groups of carolers, once called "waits," traveled around from house to house spreading the holiday spirit and singing the often ancient carols that were familiar to all who heard them. The world "carol" (in French called "noel") refers to cries of joy and good tidings as well as to song that in the thirteenth century originally accompanied a particular kind of folk dance. These songs were not of a strictly religious nature but invariably struck a note of goodwill and joy. Most of the extremely popular, well-known Christmas carols of today are more religious in theme and were for the most part written in the nineteenth century.

The Christmas tree itself, a primarily German custom, was not unknown in England before 1841, but it was on that date that Prince Albert, himself German, arranged for a Christmas tree to be set up in Windsor Castle for the delight of his wife, Queen Victoria, and the royal family. The custom promptly developed into a passion that has certainly not abated to this day.

The table at which the King [Henry VII, keeping Christmas at the Palace of Placentia at Greenwich] sat was richly decorated and groaned beneath the good fare placed upon it, for there was brawn, roast beef, venison pasty, pheasants, swan, capons, lampreys, pyke in latimer sauce, custard, partridge, fruit, plovers and a huge plum pudding which required the efforts of two men to carry. Afterwards plays were performed and there was much music and dancing, and in the large kitchens after the spit had stopped its ceaseless turning, and the King had dined . . . a merry crowd gathered. . . . and we had, besides a good chine of beef and other good cheer, eighteen mince pies in a dish. . . .

Samuel Pepys's diary,
January 6, 1662

An even more recent tradition was established after World War II. In gratitude for British help during the war, the people of Oslo, Norway, have annually sent to England a huge Norway spruce; amidst much fanfare, it is raised and copiously decorated in London's Trafalgar Square.

There is much scholarly fretting about who owns the distinction of having invented that most ubiquitous accoutrement of the holiday season, the Christmas card. Its immediate forebear was something called the Christmas piece, which generally consisted of elaborately decorated sheets of colored paper with carefully inked holiday sentiments (to show off penmanship). It is generally agreed that following the establishment of the one-penny postal service in 1840, the first commercially produced cards were offered for sale in 1846 by Sir Henry Cole.

Since the 1870's, the phenomenon of exchanging decorative cards at Christmastime has became so enormously popular that last year in Britain and the United States, over one billion cards were handled by the respective postal services of those countries.

Like many Christmas traditions, plum pudding, or in any case a near approximation of it, predates the Christian era, cropping up as a feature of the Druid Yuletide celebration. According to legend an ancient god of plenty called Daga put together the best meats, fruits, and spices on earth into a kind of a pudding in celebration of the winter solstice.

These days it is a rare plum pudding that contains any plums, but the name refers back to a time before prunes had been replaced by raisins. It started out as a kind of porridge served at the beginning of a meal, but as the dish evolved, its consistency got thicker, meat disappeared from its ingredients (except for a trace of suet), and it began to be served at the end of the meal. So rich was it that its consumption was for a time banned by the Puritans—which didn't stop the citizens of Devon from creating, in 1819, the largest plum pudding on record: nine hundred pounds.

England was merry England when
Old Christmas brought his sports again.
'Twas Christmas broach'd the mightiest ale;
'Twas Christmas told the merriest tale;
A Christmas gambol oft could cheer
The poor man's heart through half the year.

"Lochinvar"
Sir Walter Scott

A Holiday Game

A plan for amusing the young folks in an instructive fashion is to take some simple subject, such as the Christmas pudding, and let each one give his and her idea of how it is made and cooked, what the ingredients are, and where they are grown or manufactured. It is wonderful how much of interest is to be found even in a Christmas pudding, besides its pleasant taste—the growing of the raisins, currants, and candied peels, almonds, etc.; the cathedral-like salt mines from whence the salt is taken; the flour, made from golden wheat; the suet from the fat ox, and so on. This opens and expands the minds of children very much, and even the older people have to brush up their memories to reply to the questions asked on all sides.

The Housewife (1895),
a Victorian ladies' journal

Gift giving on Christmas also dates only from Victorian times. Before that it was more traditional to exchange gifts on New Year's or on Twelfth Night. An exception is the ancient and venerable tradition of Boxing Day, which takes place on the feast of St. Stephen, December 26. Traditionally, on that day the alms box in every English church is opened and the contents distributed to the poor. Perhaps for that reason it was customary for working people to open their own little "tips boxes" on that day, and it is not coincidental that Dutch and German children traditionally break open their ceramic piggy banks then.

Furminty, firmity, furmenty, fermenty, or *frumenty*? However you say it, this preparation of hulled wheat or sometimes barley was a favorite food in England for centuries. Here is a recipe from Anne Bowman's *The New Cookery Book*, 1869: "This preparation of the grains of wheat is still a common Christmas-eve supper-dish in some of the provinces. Boil a quarter of a pint of wheat in milk for three or four hours, till swelled, but not broken. Then add another quart of new milk or cream, three ounces each of sugar and currants, a stick of cinnamon, or half a grated nutmeg, and boil up a quarter of an hour; then stir in a glass of brandy, then serve in cups."

St. Stephen's Day is particularly important in Ireland, where it is the occasion for the Wren Boys' Procession. Young men dress up extravagantly, sometimes in masks, and parade about noisily with a long pole, atop which is fixed a holly bush. In the bush supposedly is a captured wren, for whose sake the young people, congue firmly in cheek, beg money.

In Scotland Christmas is a bit more soberly observed than in other parts of Britain, but the Scots more than make up for it on New Year's Eve (called Hogmanay) and New Year's Day. The name Hogmanay possibly harks back to the alliance between Scotland and France, when the French custom called Hoguinana may have been imported, or perhaps it refers more simply to a kind of oat cake that was traditionally given to children on New Year's Eve.

The other important Scottish tradition on New Year's is called first footing. The fortune, good or ill, of the inhabitants of the house are thought to depend on who first sets foot in it after the passing of the old year. Strangers are generally considered to bring good luck, especially a stranger of a particular color of hair (dark in some countries, fair in others).

Carol singing, always popular in all the British Isles, has been a particularly honored tradition in Wales, where the custom is called *eisteddfodde*. Caroling in Wales is often accompanied by a harp. In the more rural areas of Wales it is sometimes still the custom for a villager, known on this occasion as the *mari llwyd*, to prowl about the community draped in white with a horse's skull held up on a long pole. Any unwary victims given a "bite" by the horse's jaws are obliged to pay a fine.

ROAST BEEF

5- to 6-pound rib roast
Freshly ground black pepper
Fresh rosemary, finely chopped (optional)
2 cloves garlic, pressed (optional)
Salt

Preheat oven to 450°F.

Rub the beef all over with freshly ground black pepper, rosemary, and garlic, if you are using them. Place the beef in roasting pan, bone side down.

Roast for 30 minutes.

Reduce heat to 325°F. and continue roasting, 12 minutes per pound for rare, 14 or 15 minutes per pound for medium. The internal temperature for rare beef should be 120° to 125°F. and for medium, 140°F. on a meat thermometer.

Remove the roast from the oven, sprinkle with salt, and let stand for 15 minutes before carving.

Yield: 6 to 8 servings

HORSERADISH SAUCE

1 cup heavy cream
½ teaspoon sugar
½ teaspoon salt
1 tablespoon fresh lemon juice
1 heaping tablespoon or more prepared horseradish to taste

Whip the cream together with the sugar and salt until stiff. Fold in lemon juice and horseradish to taste. Serve with roast beef.

Yield: 1 cup of sauce.

Lay pretty long in bed, and then rose, leaving my wife desirous to sleep, having sat up till four this morning seeing her mayds make mince pies. I to church, where our parson Mills made a good sermon. Then home, and dined on some good ribbs of beef roasted and mince pies; only my wife, brother, and Barker, and plenty of good wine of my owne, and my heart full of true joy; and thanks to God Almighty for the goodness of my condition at this day.

Samuel Pepys's diary,
Christmas Day, 1666

YORKSHIRE PUDDING

2 large eggs
1 cup milk
1 cup all-purpose flour
½ teaspoon salt
freshly ground black pepper
2 tablespoons beef drippings

Preheat oven to 450°F. Pour out all the drippings from the roast beef and reserve, but do not wash the roasting pan.

Beat the eggs and milk together until very light and frothy. Gradually beat in the flour, salt, and 2 tablespoons of drippings.

Strain the reserved beef drippings, return to roasting pan, and place in oven for about 10 minutes, until very hot. Pour the batter into the hot roasting pan and bake for 10 minutes at 450°F. Reduce heat to 375°F. and bake about 20 minutes longer until pudding is brown and puffy.

Yield: 6 to 8 servings.

Roast Goose with Sage and Onion Stuffing

1 8- to 10-pound goose
½ teaspoon salt
4 tablespoons butter
1 large onion, finely chopped
2 stalks celery, finely diced
Liver from the goose
5 cups fresh bread crumbs
4 fresh sage leaves, chopped
or 1 teaspoon dried sage
1 teaspoon salt
Freshly ground black pepper
1 large egg

Preheat oven to 400°F.

Remove giblets from the goose. Pull away any loose fat from inside the body cavity. Rinse the goose under cold running water and pat dry with paper towels. Sprinkle with salt inside and out.

In a skillet, melt the butter and sauté the onion until it softens but does not brown (about 10 minutes). Add the celery and the goose liver and sauté about 10 minutes longer until the liver is just firm. Remove the liver and mince it.

In a large bowl mix the butter, onions and celery together with the bread crumbs. Mix in the minced goose liver and the sage. Season with salt and pepper. Beat the egg and stir it in.

Stuff the goose with the bread-crumb mixture. Truss it and sew or skewer the cavity closed. Pull the neck skin down and under the back and fasten with skewers or toothpicks. Prick the skin of the goose all over with a skewer or sharp fork. Place breast side up on a rack in a roasting pan.

Roast for 15 minutes at 400°F., then lower the temperature to 325°F. and turn breast side down and cook for 2 hours. At the end of 2 hours, turn goose breast side up again and cook another 2 hours. Test for doneness by pricking the leg close to the body. Juices should run clear. Remove from oven and let stand for 15 or 20 minutes before carving.

Yield: 8 servings.

> There never was such a goose. Bob said he didn't believe there ever was such a goose cooked. Its tenderness and flavor, size and cheapness, were themes of universal admiration. Eked out by applesauce and mashed potatoes, it was a sufficient dinner for the whole family; indeed, as Mrs. Cratchit said with great delight (surveying one small atom of a bone upon the dish), they hadn't ate it all at last! Yet every one had had enough, and the youngest Cratchits in particular were steeped in sage and onion to the eyebrows!
>
> *A Christmas Carol,*
> Charles Dickens

Lamb's Wool

This old English punch, which dates back to the Middle Ages, is said to be the one that was originally served in the wassail bowl. Perhaps the name derives from the fuzzy white baked apples that float in the bowl.

5 baking apples, cores removed
1 quart apple cider
½ teaspoon cinnamon
¼ teaspoon grated nutmeg
¼ teaspoon ginger
2 tablespoons brown sugar
1 quart dark ale

Preheat oven to 450°F.

Bake the apples in a roasting pan for about 1 hour, until they are very soft and just bursting. Remove from oven, let cool a little, and cut each apple in half.

In a large saucepan, simmer the apple cider together with the cinnamon, nutmeg, and ginger for about 15 minutes. Add the sugar and stir to dissolve. Add the dark ale and heat until hot not boiling.

Arrange the halved baked apples in a large punch bowl. Pour the hot liquid over the apples and serve warm in large mugs.

Yield: about 12 servings.

Mincemeat (With Meat)

Recipes for mincemeat, redolent with spices and liquor, were originally intended as ways to preserve meat without smoking or salting. It had another important advantage as well, thought Francis Bacon, who wrote, "Mincing of meat in pies saveth the grinding of teeth." Today you will more often come across meatless mincemeat, but the traditional mixture is delicious and worth trying. The recipe for meatless mincemeat that follows is a particular favorite and makes a wonderful pie filling.

1½ pounds very lean beef, cut into 1-inch cubes
4 cups beef broth
½ pound beef suet, finely chopped
6 Granny Smith apples, peeled, cored, and chopped
3 cups brown sugar
1 cup dark raisins
1 cup golden raisins
1½ cups currants
½ cup citron, finely chopped
½ cup candied orange peel, finely chopped
½ cup candied lemon peel, finely chopped
2 lemons with rind, seeds removed, finely chopped or ground
2 oranges, with rind, seeds removed and finely chopped or ground
2 teaspoons cinnamon
1 teaspoon mace
1 teaspoon cloves
1 teaspoon grated nutmeg
2 cups apple cider
1 cup cognac
1 cup dark rum

In a saucepan, cook the meat and beef broth adding water to cover if necessary, at a gentle simmer for 1 to 1½ hours. The meat should be tender and easy to shred. Cool meat in broth. Drain and reserve the broth and shred the beef with your hands.

In a very large saucepan, combine shredded beef, suet, reserved broth, and all the other ingredients except cognac and rum. Simmer gently for 3 hours, stirring the mixture frequently. Mincemeat should be very thick when it is done.

Turn the mincemeat into large bowl or crock and stir in the cognac and rum. This mixture can stay covered in the refrigerator for many weeks. Stir it from time to time and add more cognac or rum if it starts to dry out.

Yield: About 4 quarts, enough for 4 large pies.

Mincemeat (Without Meat)

8 Granny Smith apples, cored and quartered
1 whole orange, quartered and seeds removed
1 whole lemon, quartered and seeds removed
1½ cups dark seedless raisins
1½ cups golden raisins
1½ cups currants
½ cup candied orange peel
½ cup candied lemon peel
½ cup citron
2 cups apple cider
3 cups brown sugar
1 teaspoon cinnamon
1 teaspoon coriander
1 teaspoon mace
1 teaspoon allspice
1 teaspoon grated nutmeg
½ teaspoon salt
½ cup cognac or dark rum

Put the apples, orange, lemon, raisins, currants, candied orange peel and lemon peel, and citron through the coarse blade of a food grinder. Alternately, you can do this in your food processor, but leave the mixture rather coarse; do not overprocess.

Put the ground mixture in a large kettle, add the cider, sugar, cinnamon, coriander, mace, allspice, nutmeg, and salt. Bring to a boil, reduce heat, and simmer, stirring frequently, for 15 to 20 minutes until mixture is very thick. Transfer to a bowl or crock and stir in cognac or rum. Cover and refrigerate. This will keep several weeks in the refrigerator. Add more cognac or rum as necessary.

Yield: 12 to 16 cups, enough for 3 or 4 pies.

A health of the King and Queene here.
Nexte crowne the Bowle full
With gentle lamb's woll;
Add sugar nutmeg and ginger,
With store of ale too;
And this ye must do
To make the wassail a swinger.

Robert Herrick

Mincemeat Pie

3 cups all-purpose flour
¼ teaspoon salt
12 tablespoons unsalted butter, very cold
3 to 4 tablespoons ice water, as needed
3½ to 4 cups mincemeat
1 egg yolk mixed with 2 tablespoons water

Put the flour and salt in the bowl of a food processor and process to mix together. Cut butter into small pieces and add to flour. Process on and off until mixture resembles a coarse meal. With motor on, gradually add ice water until the mixture gathers itself into a ball. Remove the ball of dough, wrap in plastic, and refrigerate for 30 minutes.

Preheat oven to 375°F. Grease a 9-inch pie plate with butter or vegetable shortening.

Divide the dough in half and roll out on a lightly floured surface. Line the pie plate with dough. Fill with mincemeat. Roll out second half of dough and cover the pie with top crust. Seal the edges and cut a vent hole in the top. Brush with egg yolk mixed with water.

Bake for 40 to 45 minutes, until crust is golden brown. Let cool before serving.

Yield: 1 pie.

CHRISTMAS SPICED BEEF

Spiced Beef is a particular Christmas specialty of Ireland. Although it is made over a period of five days to a week, there is very little work involved. Once you try it, you may find that you include it quite often in party menus the year round. It is a very festive and unusual dish.

1 6-pound (approximately) piece of brisket or top round
1/3 cup brown sugar
1 cup coarse sea salt
2 tablespoons chopped shallots
1 tablespoon freshly ground black pepper
1 tablespoon juniper berries, slightly crushed
1 1/2 teaspoons allspice
1 1/2 teaspoons cloves
2 bay leaves, crushed
1/2 teaspoon thyme
1/2 teaspoon rosemary

For cooking:
4 medium onions, sliced
4 carrots, sliced in rounds
2 stalks celery, sliced
2 cups Guinness stout

Rub the beef all over with the brown sugar, place into a large ceramic bowl, cover, and refrigerate for 24 hours.

In a bowl, combine the salt, shallots, black pepper, juniper berries, allspice, cloves, bay leaves, and thyme. Mix well. Rub this salt mixture into the beef. Place whatever remains of the salt mixture in the bottom of the ceramic bowl, put beef on top of it, cover, and refrigerate 3 to 4 days (can be as long as a week). Turn the beef once a day and rub more of the salt mixture into it.

To cook the beef, scrape away the salt and spices and place it in a heavy Dutch oven. Pour in water just to cover. Cover and simmer very gently, so that only an occasional bubble ruffles the surface of the water for 4 to 5 hours, until the beef is very tender. Add the Guinness stout for the last hour of cooking. Cool the beef in the cooking liquid. Remove and press overnight between 2 heavy plates, the top one weighted with something heavy.

Serve cold, thinly sliced.

Yield: 12 to 14 servings.

WASSAIL BOWL

Wassail was traditionally served on all twelve days of Christmas. People too poor to make their own wassail went from door to door carrying a large wooden bowl singing carols for wassail. It was considered a great treat if you got some of the toast in your portion of wassail and most probably is the origin of the expression, "drinking a toast."

3 quarts ale or dark beer
1 bottle sweet sherry
1 cup cognac (optional)
2 cups brown sugar
1 lemon, sliced
1 teaspoon powdered ginger
1 teaspoon grated nutmeg
10 slices white bread, crusts removed, toasted, buttered, and quartered

In a large saucepan, gently heat the beer, sherry, and cognac, if using, but do not boil. Add the sugar, lemon and ginger and cook over very low heat, stirring, until the sugar is completely dissolved. Pour into a punch bowl and float toast on the surface before serving. Alternately pass the toast on a separate platter so people can dip it into the drink.

Yield: about 20 servings.

VARIATION: Beat six eggs until very light and frothy. Beat the eggs into the hot liquid just before serving.

PLUM PUDDING

This is a somewhat lighter version of the traditional Christmas pudding so beloved of the Cratchits.

1 cup pitted prunes, coarsely chopped
1 cup dark raisins, coarsely chopped
1 cup golden raisins, coarsely chopped
1 cup currants
¼ cup candied orange peel, coarsely chopped
¼ cup candied lemon peel, coarsely chopped
½ cup cognac, dark rum or Madeira

> ***Plum Pudding***
>
> Now Mrs. Cratchit left the room alone—too nervous to bear witnesses—to take the pudding up, and bring it in. Suppose it should not be done enough! Suppose it should break in turning it out! Suppose somebody should have stolen it, while they were merry with the goose—a supposition at which the two young Cratchits became livid!
>
> "Hallo! A great deal of steam! The pudding was out of the copper. In half a minute Mrs. Cratchit entered—flushed, but smiling proudly—with the pudding, like a speckled cannonball, blazing in ignited brandy, with Christmas holly stuck into the top.
>
> "Oh, a wonderful pudding! Bob Cratchit said that he regarded it as the greatest success achieved by Mrs. Cratchit since their marriage.
>
> *A Christmas Carol*
> Charles Dickens

1½ cups stout, dark ale or beer
¼ pound beef suet, finely minced
1 cup brown sugar
4 large eggs
1 teaspoon cinnamon
½ grated nutmeg
¼ teaspoon cloves
¼ teaspoon allspice
Juice and grated rind of 1 lemon
Grated rind of 1 orange
½ cup blanched slivered almonds
2 Granny Smith, or other tart apples, peeled, cored, and coarsely chopped
1 cup fine bread crumbs
1 cup sifted all-purpose flour
1½ teaspoons baking powder
½ teaspoon baking soda
½ teaspoon salt

Butter for pudding bowl
¾ cup cognac for flaming
Sprig of holly
Hard Sauce (next recipe)

In a large bowl combine the prunes, raisins, currants, candied orange peel, and candied lemon peel. Mix together with ½ cup cognac, rum, or Madeira and the stout, ale, or beer. Cover and let stand for several hours to plump up the fruit.

Cream together the suet and sugar until very light and fluffy. Beat in the eggs, one at a time, until mixture is very frothy and pale lemon-colored. Stir in the fruit and all the liquid. Stir cinnamon, nutmeg, cloves, allspice, lemon juice and lemon rind and grated orange rind. Stir in almonds, apples, and bread crumbs.

Sift the flour together with the baking powder, baking soda, and salt. Stir into the liquid mixture and mix well.

Butter the insides of a 2-quart pudding mold or bowl, or two 1-quart pudding molds or bowls. Spoon the pudding mixture into molds or bowls. Cover tightly with buttered aluminum foil. Drape a dampened kitchen towel over each mold or bowl and tie it in place with a long piece of kitchen cord.

Place on a rack inside a large kettle. Pour in enough boiling water to come two-thirds up the sides of the pudding mold. Cover the kettle and steam the pudding for 4 to 5 hours. Add boiling water as needed to maintain the water level.

To serve immediately, remove the cover and let stand for 10 minutes before unmolding. Invert the pudding on a large serving platter. Stick holly sprig into center of pudding. Heat the ¾ cup cognac, light it, and pour it over the pudding while it is burning. Serve with Hard Sauce.

Yield: 10 to 12 servings.

NOTE: The pudding can be stored covered for months in the refrigerator. Steam for 1 hour before serving.

Leftover pudding can be fried in butter and served with Hard Sauce.

HARD SAUCE

1 stick unsalted butter, at room temperature
1 cup confectioners' sugar
1 egg white
2 tablespoons cognac or rum

Cream the butter with the sugar until very light and fluffy. Beat the egg white separately until fluffy but not stiff, then beat into the butter mixture. Finally, beat in the cognac or rum.

Makes about 1 cup.

IRISH GINGERBREAD CAKE

Rich with spices, dates, and walnuts, this dense confection is more like a fruitcake than a gingerbread. It is delicious straight from the oven but gets even better if allowed to rest for three or four days before eating. Wrap it well and keep it in an airtight tin or plastic box in a cool place. It makes a wonderful gift and is delicious served with tea or dessert.

4 cups all-purpose flour
1 teaspoon baking soda
2 teaspoons ginger
2 teaspoons cinnamon
1 teaspoon cloves
½ teaspoon grated nutmeg
1 cup shelled walnuts, coarsely chopped
½ cup dark raisins
½ cup pitted dates, coarsely chopped
3 knobs candied ginger, coarsely chopped
1 cup butter
½ cup molasses
½ cup honey
1 cup brown sugar
¼ cup Scotch whiskey
4 large eggs

Preheat oven to 350°F.

Grease an 8-inch square pan with butter and line the bottom with baking parchment.

Sift the flour, baking soda, ginger, cinnamon, cloves, and nutmeg into a large mixing bowl. Stir in the walnuts, raisins, dates, and candied ginger.

Melt the butter over low heat and stir in molasses, brown sugar, and Scotch whiskey. Remove from heat and when slightly cooled, stir in the eggs. Stir the liquid mixture into the flour and spices. Spoon the cake mixture into the buttered cake pan and smooth the surface with a spatula. Bake for 20 minutes at 350°F. Lower the oven temperature to 300°F. and bake 2 hours, until a cake tester inserted in the center comes out clean. Allow gingerbread to cool in the pan for about 20 minutes. Remove from pan, strip off parchment paper, cut into small squares, and serve.

Yield: 1 gingerbread cake.

Symbolic Items to Include in a Twelfth Night or New Year's Cake

A button or ring will bring faithfullness.
A coin will bring wealth.
A bean or pea will bring wisdom.
A thimble will bring patience.
A paper heart will bring devotion.
A clove confers the status of fool or court jester.

TWELFTH DAY CAKE

A deliciously sweet cake to bring the Christmas season to a close. Be sure to bury a bean and a pea inside the cake, so as to designate your king and queen for the day. See page 28 to find out other favors to hide in the cake and to learn their significance.

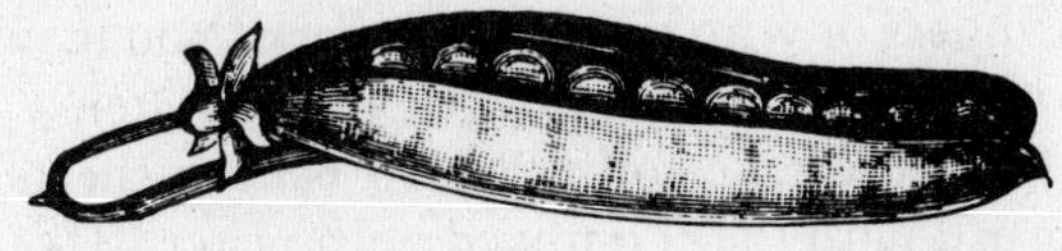

½ cup rum
1 cup golden raisins
1 cup currants
1 cup seedless dark raisins
2 sticks unsalted butter, softened to room temperature
1 cup sugar
4 large eggs
½ teaspoon cinnamon
¼ teaspoon nutmeg
¼ teaspoon mace
Grated rind of 1 lemon
1 dried pea
1 dried bean
½ cup blanched almonds, roughly chopped
3 cups flour, approximately
Fancy Sugar Icing, page 120

In a bowl, combine the rum with the raisins and currants. Let stand for several hours. Drain the fruit and reserve the rum.

Preheat oven to 275°F. Grease a 10-inch cake that is at least 3 inches deep with butter or vegetable shortening. Line it with baking parchment.

Cream the butter and sugar together until very light and fluffy. Beat in eggs one at a time until mixture is very light and frothy. Beat in 3 tablespoons of the reserved rum and stir in the cinnamon, nutmeg, mace, and grated lemon rind. Stir in the pea and the bean. Stir in the almonds and the flour and mix well to make a smooth batter.

Spoon the batter into prepared cake pan and bake at 275°F. for about 2 hours, or until cake tester comes out clean. Let cool in cake pan until just warm. Turn cake out onto cooling rack and peel away baking parchment. When completely cool spread top with Fancy Sugar Icing.

Yield: 1 cake.

BISHOP'S CUP

Fine oranges,
Well, roasted, with sugar and wine in a cup,
They'll make a sweet Bishop when gentlefolks sup.

Dean Jonathan Swift

2 oranges
12 cloves
1 cup water
6 allspice berries
1 1-inch stick of cinnamon
2 slices of fresh ginger
1 strip of lemon peel
½ cup brown sugar
2 bottles of port
¼ cup brandy or cognac
Freshly grated nutmeg

Preheat oven to 300°F.

Stick each orange with 6 cloves and roast in a baking pan in the oven for 45 minutes. Remove and when cool enough to handle, cut oranges into quarters.

Place the water, allspice, cinnamon, ginger, lemon peel, and sugar in a saucepan and bring to a boil. Simmer until mixture has reduced by about ⅓. Place water and spices in a large punch bowl together with the quartered roasted oranges. Heat the port and brandy in a large enameled saucepan until hot, but do not boil. Combine with oranges and spice syrup in punch bowl. Serve hot, sprinkled with freshly grated nutmeg.

Yield: 10 to 12 servings.

COVENTRY GODCAKES

In Coventry on New Year's Day it is a long-time custom for children to call on their godparents. For this good behavior the children are blessed and are given these delicious triangular (in honor of the Trinity) godcakes to eat with their tea.

For the pastry:

2 cups flour
½ teaspoon salt
1 teaspoon sugar
1 stick unsalted butter, very cold
1 large egg
1 to 2 tablespoons ice water

Filling:

4 tablespoons unsalted butter, at room temperature
¼ cup brown sugar
¾ cup currants
3 tablespoons candied lemon peel, finely chopped
3 tablespoons candied orange peel, finely chopped
½ teaspoon cinnamon
½ teaspoon nutmeg
½ teaspoon allspice
1 egg beaten with 1 tablespoon water

Place the flour, salt, and sugar in the bowl of a food processor. Pulse on and off to mix the ingredients. Cut the butter into small pieces and with the processor on add it to the flour. This will make a mixture resembling a coarse meal. Beat the egg with 1 tablespoon of ice water. With the processor on, add the egg to the flour mixture. Add additional ice water if necessary to make a dough that forms into a ball in the food processor bowl. Turn off, remove the dough, wrap in plastic and refrigerate for 30 minutes to an hour. (This can be done a day or two ahead.)

Preheat oven to 325°F. Grease 2 baking sheets with butter or vegetable shortening.

Prepare the filling. Cream the butter and sugar together until very light and fluffy. Stir in the currants, candied lemon peel, candied orange peel, cinnamon, nutmeg and allspice.

Roll out the pastry dough on a lightly floured board or pastry cloth until it is less than ¼ inch thick. Cut the dough into 4-inch squares. (Reroll the scraps and cut into more squares.) Place 1 heaping teaspoon of filling in one corner of a pastry square and fold over from corner to corner to make a triangle. Seal the edges with your fingers or with the tines of a fork. You may need to moisten the edges with a little water.

Place the cakes on prepared baking sheets and brush with the egg mixed with water. Bake for 15 minutes, until pastry is golden brown. Cool before serving.

Yield: 12 to 14 Godcakes.

ATHOLE BROSE

Athole is a mountainous region of Scotland that gave birth to this ancient Scot's brew or "brose." Originally it was made with whiskey and oatmeal gruel, but today the gruel has been replaced with honey. Athole Brose is traditionally served on New Year's Eve, or Hogmanay. It is also considered to be an excellent cure for colds.

1½ cups honey
2 cups heavy cream
2 cups Scotch whiskey

In a heavy saucepan heat the honey until it begins to thin out. Add the heavy cream and heat gently but do not boil. Remove from heat and stir in the whiskey.

Serve hot or very cold.

Yield: 4 to 6 servings.

THE CHRISTMAS TREE, EVERGREENS, AND OTHER PAGAN TRADITIONS

Even in our relatively unsuperstitious modern times, the dark and dreary days of winter leave many of us with the feeling that spring is simply too far off. For us, perhaps no less than for our ancestors, the evergreen is a powerful symbol of the regenerative powers of nature. In fact, the Christmas tree and its forerunners, as well as other forms of midwinter greenery, have been a central part of religious and festive customs since the earliest human cultures.

The Christmas tree as we know it today represents the blending of several traditions. In medieval Germany it was once the custom during Advent, the four Sundays before Christmas, to put on religious plays about Adam and Eve and the Great Fall. Onstage there was invariably a tree representing the tree of life (from which Adam and Eve ate the fruit and thus were expelled from Eden). That tree, called the Paradise Tree, became quite popular apart from the plays, and many feel that it was the direct ancestor of our modern Christmas tree.

It is also said that St Boniface of Crediton (an English missionary in Germany during the eighth century) chopped down a sacred oak beneath which human sacrifices had been made. The story goes that when the oak fell, a young fir tree sprang up in its place. Overwhelmed by the symbolism, the saint suggested the fir tree as an emblem of the new faith.

Traditional stories notwithstanding, decorated trees of one sort or another played a part in winter rituals long before the Christian Era. The ancient Egyptians brought small specimens of the green date palm into their homes as symbols of immortality, the Romans trimmed their trees with treats and trinkets for the Saturnalia, and the Druids honored Odin by tying fruits and other offerings onto the branches of trees.

O Christmas tree, O Christmas tree
How lovely are your branches.
In summer sun, in winter snow,
A dress of green you always show.
O Christmas tree, O Christmas tree,
How lovely are your branches.

O Christmas tree, O Christmas tree,
With happiness we greet you.
When decked with candles once a year,
You fill our hearts with Yuletide cheer.
O Christmas tree, O Christmas tree,
With happiness we greet you.

Traditional German carol

The Germans believe it was Martin Luther who first decorated a Christmas tree. Out for a walk on a fine clear Christmas Eve, he was so moved by the display of stars that upon returning home he attached candles to the branches of an uprooted fir tree. While Luther may not have been literally the first to put candles on a tree, it certainly was among the Germans that the Christmas tree first achieved its current status as a primary symbol of Christmas. The practice developed from there, becoming fairly widespread by 1604. It got a big boost in England during Victorian times because of the influence of Prince Albert, who was a German prince.

> The Christmas tree with lights is gleaming,
> And stands in bright and festive glow.
> As if to say—Mark well my meaning,
> Hope's image green and bright I show.
>
> German carol

There are also quite a number of legends and superstitions surrounding the holly plant. According to one, Christ's crown of thorns was wound with holly, and after the crucifixion its white berries turned blood red. Belief in this miracle, especially in England and France, led to the tradition of hanging holly over doorways to show that the spirit was alive within. To early Christians in Northern Europe, holly is also said to symbolize Mary's love for God. In the Middle Ages, Germans thought that a sprig of the plant taken from church decorations would protect them against lightning.

Believed to have concealed the Holy

Family on their flight into Egypt, the juniper is honored at Christmastime and considered a tree of refuge. In many areas people used to smear juniper sap over their houses and stables to keep away evil spirits. In Italy, sprigs of it were hung on doors in the beguiling belief that any witch who sought to enter the home would always pause to count the leaves. It was hoped that, finding the job impossible, she would wander off without fulfilling her original (presumably evil) purpose.

Mistletoe, as a fixture of Christmas decoration, is also known as the kissing bush, an idea whose origins can be traced back to the legends of the Aesir, the Norse gods. It seems that Loki, the trickster god, used an arrow made of the wood of the mistletoe plant to slay the sun god, Balder, causing great consternation among the other gods. Together they contrived to revive Balder and

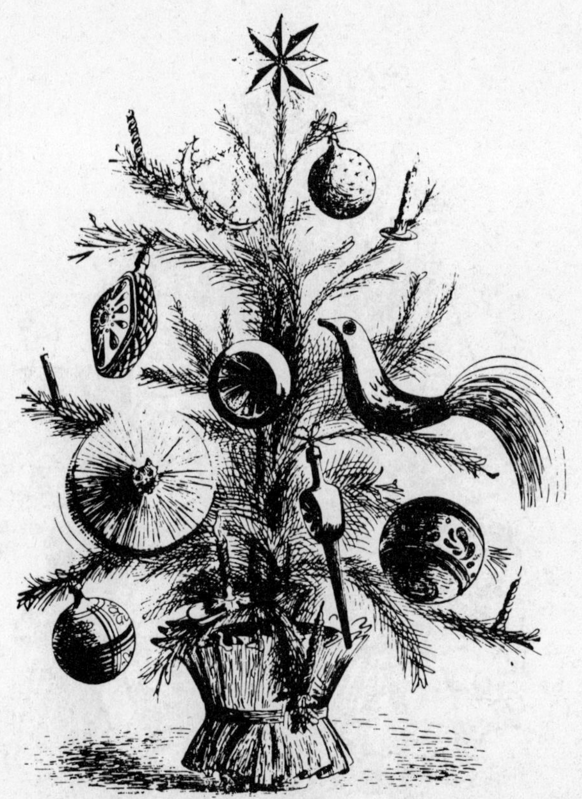

I have been looking on, this evening, at a merry company of children assembled round that pretty German toy, a Christmas Tree. The tree was planted in the middle of a great round table, and towered high above their heads. It was brilliantly lighted by a multitude of little tapers; and everywhere sparkled and glittered with bright objects. There were rosy-cheeked dolls, hiding behind green leaves; and there were real watches (with moveable hands, at least, and an endless capacity for being wound up) dangling from innumerable twigs; there were French polished tables, chairs, bedsteads, eight-day clocks, and various other articles of domestic furniture (wonderfully made in tin) perched amoung the boughs, as if in preparation for some fairy housekeeping; there were jolly, broad-face little men, much more agreeable in appearance than many real men—and no wonder, for their heads took off and showed them to be full of sugarplums; there were fiddles and drums, there were tambourines, books, work boxes, there were trinkets for the elder girls, far brighter than any grown-up gold and jewels; there were baskets and pincushions in all devices; there were guns, swords and banners, there were witches standing in enchanted rings of pasteboard, to tell fortunes; there were teetotums, humming tops, needle cases, pen wipers, smelling bottles, conversation cards, bouquet holders, real fruit, made artificially dazzling with gold leaf; imitation apples, pears, walnuts crammed with surprises; in short, as a pretty child before me delightedly whispered to another pretty child, her bosom friend, "There was everything and more."

"A Christmas Tree,"
Charles Dickens

From The Illustrated London News, *1848*

The Christmas Tree is annually prepared by her Majesty's command for the Royal children. . . . The tree employed for this festive purpose is a young fir of about eight feet high, and has six tiers of branches. On each tier, or branch, are arranged a dozen wax tapers. Pendant from the branches are elegant trays, baskets, bonbonnieres, and other receptacles for sweetmeats of the most varied and expensive kind; and of all forms, colours, and degrees of beauty. Fancy cakes, gilt gingerbread and eggs filled with sweetmeats, are also suspended by variously-coloured ribbons from the branches. The tree, which stands upon a table covered with white damask, is supported at the root by piles of sweets of a larger kind, and by toys and dolls of all descriptions, suited to the youthful fancy. . . . On the summit of the tree stands the small figure of an angel, with outstretched wings, holding in each hand a wreath.

everyone was so relieved that the mistletoe tree swore never to be an agent of evil again. Perhaps the joy that everyone felt when the sun returned is echoed by the joyous tradition of kissing beneath the mistletoe.

Mistletoe was always central to Druid rituals. The arch Druid, using a golden sickle, would snip the bough of mistletoe from its host tree sometime in November. It was to be caught in a white cloth by virgins before touching the ground. After prayers and sacrifices, the bough was divided into small pieces and distributed to the people, who took it home and hung it over their door as a talisman for fertility, healing, and as a prophylactic against witchcraft. Later tradition says that the mistletoe, a vine, was once a tree until its wood was used for the cross. From then on it became a parasite, unable to grow straight and tall on its own.

Kissing under the mistletoe is a distinctly English tradition that may go back to mistletoe's standing as a fertility fetish. In any case, the belief was that each time a kiss is claimed under the mistletoe, one of the white berries must be removed, so that when there were no more berries the kissing was to stop.

If in midwinter people yearn for spring, then light itself, no less than greenery, is an apt symbol of that hope for renewal. And lights have always been a part of midwinter celebrations, even before the ancient Jewish festival of lights, Chanukah, which takes

place at that time of year. In medieval times people constructed pyramids of burning candles to symbolize Christ as the light of the world. Eventually, Christmas trees with candles attached to their boughs replaced the pyramids, and today, for reasons of safety, electric lights have replaced the candles, but the central aspect of the symbolism is the light that banishes not just physical darkness, but emotional gloom as well. In many countries it is the custom to put a lighted candle in the windows on Christmas Eve, as a symbolic beacon for the Holy Family in their wanderings, and by extension as a sign to any lonely traveler that a welcome awaits.

In the nineteenth century, the Christmas season found Western Europe ablaze with lights—no less so than today, really, despite the absence then of electricity. In Spanish cities, groups of children meandered through the streets carrying lamps on poles to light the way for the three kings on Epiphany Eve. In Italy, the ornate Nativity scenes that graced every church, every town square, and nearly every home were all aglow with candlelight. In Germany homes were kept quite dark on Christmas Eve, the better to dazzle the children with the brilliance of the candles on the Christmas tree. In Sweden, at some risk to their hair, young girls wear a crown of candles on St. Lucia's day in early December. In France the *bûche de Noël*, a cake made to look like a Yule log, was ceremoniously ignited (flambéed) as the family prayed, and on the great boulevards of Paris every shop window shone.

Holly and Ivy

The holly and the ivy,
When they are both full grown,
Of all the trees that are in the wood,
The holly wears the crown.

The rising of the sun
And the running of the deer,
The playing of the merry organ,
Sweet singing of the choir.

A CHRISTMAS SCENT

You can easily make your house smell like Christmas. In a saucepan, combine the peels of 2 oranges, 3 cinnamon sticks, 12 whole cloves and 2½ cups water. Simmer very gently on a back burner of the stove and be sure to add more water as it evaporates.

POMANDER BALLS

These are not edible but they are very decorative and extremely fragrant. As they are quite inexpensive to make, you can make enough to hang one in each closet, pile a bunch in a bowl for a beautiful room freshener, and of course hang them from the Christmas tree. These also make excellent gifts and stocking stuffers.

Apples | *Whole cloves*
Oranges | *Cinnamon*
Lemon | *Orris root (optional)**

Press apples, oranges, and/or lemons with whole cloves so the whole fruit is entirely covered. This is a pefect family occupation while watching humdrum television. Do one at a time and complete an entire fruit before you go on to the next. Place clove-studded fruit in a paper bag with powdered cinnamon and orris root, if using, and shake well. Place powdered fruit on waxed paper in an out-of-the-way corner and let dry for about 2 weeks. Fruit will shrink as it dries. Tie with ribbon.

*Try a good pharmacy or order from Caprilands Herb Farm, Silver Street, Coventry, Conn. 06238.

You can decorate an entire Christmas tree with edible ornaments, as was often done at the turn of the century. Cookies make enchanting Christmas tree decorations: Almost all of the cookies in the Santa Claus chapter, page 107 are suitable for hanging on your Christmas tree as decorations. Roll the dough out a little thicker than called for in the recipe and be sure to prick a hole in each cookie with a knitting needle before baking. Wait until cookies are completely cool before threading some string through the cookie hole. Dental floss is excellent for this purpose.

The Christmas wreath is another tradition that has its origin in pagan custom. For Christians, however, its circular shape symbolizes God's eternal love, and its greenery signified Christ's immortality—his victory over death.

A Christmas Alphabet

A for the Animals out in the stable.
B for the Babe in his manger for cradle.
C for the Carols so blithe and gay.
D for December, the twenty-fifth day.
E for the Eve when we're all so excited.
F for the Fire when the Yule Log is lighted.
G is the Goose which you all know is fat.
H for the Holly you stick in your hat.
I for the Ivy which clings to the wall.
J is for Jesus the cause of it all.
K for the Kindness begot by this feast.
L is the Light shining way in the East.
M for the Misteltoe. Beware where it hangs!
N is the Nowell the angels first sang.
O for the Oxen, the first to adore Him.
P for the Presents wise men laid before Him.
Q for the Queerness that this should have been, near two thousand years before you were seen.
R for the Romps and Raisins and Nuts.
S for the Stocking that Santa Claus stuffs.
T for the Toys on the Christmas Tree hanging.
U is for Us over all the world ranging.
V for the Visitors welcomed so warmly.
W for the Waifs at your door singing heartily!
XYZ bother me! all I can say
This is the end of my Christmas lay.
So now to you all, wherever you may be,
A merry merry Christmas, and may many you see!

SUGARPLUMS

1 pound dried figs
1 pound pitted dates
1 pound seedless raisins
¼ pound blanched almonds
¼ pound unsalted, shelled pistachio nuts (not red)
¼ pound shelled walnuts
¼ pound macadamia nuts
¼ pound crystallized ginger
Grated rind of 2 oranges
3 tablespoons fresh lemon juice, approximately
Confectioners' sugar

Put the dried fruits and nuts through the coarse blade of a meat grinder, or process in the bowl of a food processor to a coarse mince. Place in a bowl and mix with orange rind and enough lemon juice for the mixture to stick together. Shape and roll into balls about 1 inch in diameter, and roll in confectioners' sugar. Wrap each ball in colored cellophane or colored foil and tie with a ribbon.

Yield: enough for 1 Christmas tree.

Apples, oranges, pears, lemons, tangerines, and lady apples—all make lovely tree decorations. So do the following:

Chocolate kisses
Pretzels
Miniature Hershey bars
Miniature boxes of raisins
Candy canes
Lollipops
Animal crackers

CHRISTMAS TREE GINGERBREAD

1 cup butter or margarine
1 cup brown sugar
3 large eggs
1½ cups molasses
1 tablespoon ginger
1½ teaspoons cinnamon
1 teaspoon cloves
6 cups all-purpose flour
1½ teaspoons baking soda
1½ teaspoons salt

Cream butter or margarine and sugar together until very light and fluffly. Beat in eggs, one at a time, then beat in molasses. Stir in ginger, cinnamon, and cloves. Sift flour together with baking soda and salt and stir into the creamed mixture to make a smooth dough. Scoop up into a ball, wrap in plastic, and chill in refrigerator for several hours or overnight.

Preheat oven to 350°F. Grease several cookie sheets with butter or vegetable shortening.

Roll out the dough, not too thin, on a lightly floured surface. Cut into your favorite shapes to hang on tree. Arrange on prepared cookie sheets and prick a hole with a skewer or knitting needle near top of each cookie (for string to hang from tree). Bake for 12 to 15 minutes until cookies are dry but not too crisp.

Cool on wire racks. Decorate with White Sugar Icing, page 115 or Fancy Sugar Icing, page 120.

Yield: 3 to 4 dozen cookies, depending on size.

And may your happiness ever spread
Like butter on hot gingerbread.

A Traditional Couplet.

Most of the cookies on nineteenth-century Christmas trees were thicker than today's cookies: Spice, butter, and gingerbread cookies were often half an inch thick. White cookies were frequently sprinkled with red sugar, "for pretty," as the Pennsylvania Dutch still say. Cookie-baking binges often lasted for two solid weeks early in December. A "washbasketful" was a standard of measure for cookies in Pennsylvania Dutch kitchens. The housewife who didn't have at least several washbaskets full of cookies just wasn't ready for Christmas.

The Christmas Tree Book
Phillip V. Snyder

MARZIPAN

Marzipan is the perfect medium for the amateur sculptor and other budding artists. Use a small knife and your imagination to make whatever shapes your heart desires.

4 ounces almond paste
½ cup confectioners' sugar
1 tablespoon light corn syrup
Food coloring, as needed

In a small bowl, break up the almond paste with a fork. Use your hands to knead in the sugar and corn syrup. Form the dough into a smooth ball and into separate balls for different colors. Knead 1 or 2 drops of a color into each ball of dough. Sculpt into desired shapes and let dry overnight. Makes about 1 cup of marzipan.

Christmas Fudge

3 ounces unsweetened cooking chocolate
2 cups sugar
2/3 cup evaporated milk
2 tablespoons corn syrup
1/4 teaspoon salt
4 tablespoons butter
1 teaspoon vanilla extract

Break up the chocolate squares and put them in a heavy saucepan together with the sugar, milk, corn syrup and salt. Cook over low heat, stirring constantly, until it comes to a boil. This takes 15 to 20 minutes. Continue cooking on low heat until a candy thermometer reads 234°F. Remove from heat, stir in butter and let cool until it is lukewarm. Stir in vanilla and keep stirring the fudge for about 5 minutes, until the fudge begins to lose its gloss. Pour the fudge into a buttered cake pan and let stand until completely cool. Cut into bars or squares and wrap each piece in colored cellophane or aluminum foil.

Yield: about 1 pound of fudge.

One special pleasure afforded by these old-fashioned edible Christmas-tree decorations has been all but lost to us today. Traditionally, the tantalizing cookies and sweetmeats that hung on the tree were forbidden fruit, and were supposed to stay in place until the tree was taken down on Twelfth Night, when they could finally be eaten. Therefore, the inevitable final dismantling, so disappointing to today's children, was once an exciting, anticipated, and delicious climax to the Christmas season.

The Christmas Tree Book,
Phillip V. Snyder

Chocolate Fondue

3 ounces semisweet chocolate, broken into pieces
1/2 cup evaporated milk
2 tablespoons brandy or orange liqueur

In the top of a double boiler melt the chocolate over boiling water. Stir in evaporated milk and cook, stirring until well blended. Remove from heat and stir in brandy or liqueur.

Serve a fondue dip for cut-up pound cake, fruits, or marshmallows.

Yield: 6 servings.

VARIATION: Dip any shape Christmas cookies, gingerbread men, or even animal crackers into chocolate fondue and dry on waxed paper in refrigerator overnight. Hang from Christmas tree.

Popcorn Balls

2/3 cup sugar
1/2 cup water
2 1/2 tablespoons light corn syrup
1/8 teaspoon salt
1/3 teaspoon vinegar
6 cups popped corn

In a saucepan combine sugar, water, corn syrup, salt, and vinegar. Bring to a boil and reduce heat to a simmer. Cover and let cook for about 5 minutes, until the steam has washed down the sides of the pan. Uncover and cook without stirring until mixture registers 290°F. on candy thermometer.

Put the popped corn in a large bowl. Pour the hot syrup over the popped corn kernels and stir with a wooden spoon until well coated. When popcorn is cool enough to handle, rub your hands with oil or butter and shape popped corn into balls. Let cool completely. Wrap in clear or colored cellophane and hang from tree.

Yield: approximately twelve 2-inch balls.

POPCORN

Today there are special electric popcorn poppers for the home, and popcorn kernels to pop in the microwave. But all popcorn is easy to make, and without special equipment anyone can make perfectly delicious perfectly popped corn at home in just a few minutes. Use either a heavy skillet with a lid or a large pot with a lid. I use the same pot I cook spaghetti in. If you are using an electric popper or microwave popcorn, follow the manufacturer's directions.

2 tablespoons vegetable oil
½ cup popcorn kernels

Put the oil in a skillet or large pot and place on high heat. Wait 1 minute and drop in one or two kernels of corn. If the kernels pop, add the rest of the corn kernels. Cover the skillet or pot and shake the pan to move the corn kernels around. The lid should fit loosely enough for the steam to escape as the corn pops. Continue cooking and shaking until all the popping sounds slow down—about 2 or 3 minutes. Remove from heat and pour popcorn into a large serving bowl.

Yield: 6 to 8 cups popped corn.

With a large needle and strong thread string chains of popped corn kernels together and hang these from the tree. The same technique with cranberries makes beautiful red chains. Or else, alternate cranberries and popped corn kernels for a red-and-white effect.

POPCORN-MARSHMALLOW BALLS

4 tablespoons butter or margarine
1 1-pound bag marshmallows
6 quarts popped corn
Food coloring or dry fruit Jell-O (colors of your choice)
Optional candy decorations: M&M's, chocolate chips, cinnamon candies, colored sprinkles

Melt the butter or margarine in a saucepan. Add the marshmallows and cook over low heat, stirring until the marshmallows have melted and the mixture is smooth. Add a few drops of food coloring or 2 tablespoons dry fruit Jell-O, if desired. These are also nice left white like snowballs.

Pour the marshmallow mixture over the popcorn in a large bowl. Let it cool down somewhat, then mix with your hands until all the popcorn is well coated. Shape into balls and press candy decorations into the balls while they are still warm.

Wrap in clear cellophane and tie with ribbons. Hang from tree.

Yield: about twenty-five 2-inch balls.

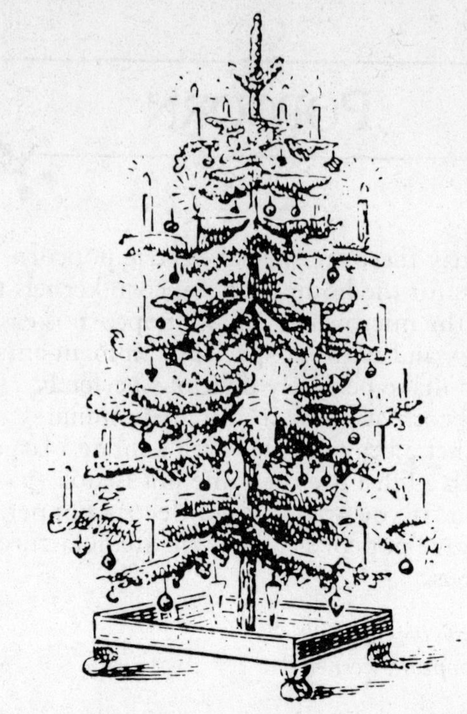

CONSOLATION BARS

Buy a selection of tissue paper in different colors and wrap small chocolate bars, preferably imported from Switzerland, in tissue paper and tie with ribbons. Hang these from the tree and eat them as a consolation prize when you dismantle the tree.

CHRISTMAS IN FRANCE

In France Christmas celebrations center on the *crèche* or manger scene. In nearly every French home at Christmastime as well as in churches and public gathering places, there will be a Nativity setting, often composed of tiny clay figures called *santons*, or little saints. Especially popular in the south of France, these brightly painted images are made by local craftsmen during the year and are often seen for sale at the famous Christmas fairs at Marseilles and Aix. The level of craftsmanship involved in the making of these figures is sometimes quite astounding, and these skills are proudly handed down from one generation to the next.

Historically, the manger scene, which is said to have been created first by St. Francis in the thirteenth century, was popularized in France a century later when the Papacy temporarily moved to Avignon from Rome. By 1800, figurines imported from Italy called *santi belli* inspired French craftsmen to begin producing their own—often with more concern for self-expression than for historical accuracy. It's not uncommon in French crèches to see clay likenesses of local dignitaries and characters displayed side by side with the more traditional figures of the Christ Child, the animals of the manger, and the three wise men.

In Provence especially, children regard making the crèche as their particular contribution to the Christmas festivities. They are often ingenious in their use of mosses, lichen, small branches, and pebbles to create the scenes that resemble the rocky olive-covered hills of their own region. Models of red-tiled village inns and stables filled with hay make a charming background for the santons.

The Christmas tree, on the other hand, has never been particularly popular in France, and the Yule log, though once important, is now mostly diregarded. It is remembered, however, in the name and shape of the traditional French Christmas cake, the *bûche de Noël*.

In sheep-raising regions, the Christmas service is also called the festival of shepherds. At the church of St. Michel-de-Frigolet in

In historical terms, it can be said that the first Christmas celebration in France was held in 496, when St. Remi, the bishop of Rheims, chose the day of the Nativity to baptize Clovis I and his army.

Les Baux, Provence, men and women dressed in traditional shepherd's costume parade around the church carrying a newborn lamb. The lamb, a common symbol of Christ's innocence, is laid in a gaily decorated cart drawn by a ram; the procession circles the church three times, accompanied by flute and drum. Before the congregation takes communion, a child offers the ritual lamb to the priest.

Epiphany or Twelfth Night

The holiday now celebrated as the feast of the Epiphany, also called the feast of kings, Twelfth Night, or the last day of Christmas, originated in Egypt during the third century as a pagan festival celebrated at the winter solstice in honor of the Egyptian sun god. Eventually many of the trappings of the festival were taken over by Christians who wished to celebrate the manifestation, or epiphaneia, of the Savior's divinity. They celebrated not only Christ's birth but also the visit and adoration of the Magi, and soon Epiphany commemorated Christ's baptism in the River Jordan as a third important manifestation of divinity. The feast was taken up by the Western Church in the fourth century, at nearly the same time that Christmas—known then only as the feast of Christ's Nativity—was also becoming accepted as a holiday.

It is a common custom in many cultures, derived from the traditions of the Roman Saturnalia, to bake a cake with a trinket or bean hidden in it. The person who finds it in his portion becomes the lord of the feast. Sometimes two trinkets are hidden—one for a king and one for a queen. In the royal courts of the late Middle Ages, these customs became enormously popular, although the Roman theme of lordship of the feast had long since been subsumed to the more Christian themes of Christ's kingship and of the adoring Magi.

Le réveillon, the grandest feast of an already festive season, is a late supper held after midnight Mass on Christmas Eve. Since every region of France has its own highly developed culinary traditions, the menu for *le réveillon* understandably varies from place to place. In Alsace, custom calls for goose as a main course; in Brittany, buckwheat cakes with sour cream are a must, in Burgundy the people feast on turkey with chestnuts, and in Paris on oysters and pâté de foie gras.

After dinner and just before bedtime (for Christmas Eve is generally a very, very long day) the children set out their shoes by the fireside in the hope that they will be filled with presents from Père Noël, literally, Father Christmas, a figure more and more like our Santa Claus, or else from *le petit Noël* (the name means "little Christmas" and refers to the Christ Child). At one time the shoes would have been the traditional wooden shoes called *sabots*, though these days anything, including Nike running shoes, is probably acceptable. Adults, incidentally, generally wait until New Year's Day to exchange their presents.

On Christmas Day there might be a puppet show or Nativity play to divert restless children, and for weary adults it is generally a day of well-earned rest.

The celebration of Twelfth Night has a particularly rich and controversial history in France, centered on the custom of serving special cakes, some portion of which contained a bean. The lucky finder of the bean was declared king for a day and the result was a kind of (mostly) playful anarchy and

the suspension of the normal rules of sexual and social decorum that has accompanied this very ancient tradition since even before the Roman Saturnalia.

Though by the seventeenth century the custom was almost exclusively associated with the celebration of Twelfth Night, and the celebration of Twelfth Night was by then a thoroughly Christian rite, the choosing of a bean king came under attack as a pagan practice—offensive, some thought, to both the church and the real king.

> Now when Jesus was born in Bethlehem of Judaea in the days of Herod the king, behold there came wise men from the east to Jerusalem, Saying, Where is he that is born King of the Jews? for we have seen his star in the east, and are come to worship him. . . .
>
> Then Herod, when he had privily called the wise men, inquired of them diligently what time the star appeared.
>
> And he sent them to Bethlehem, and said, Go and search diligently for the young child; and when ye have found him, bring me word again, that I may come and worship him also.
>
> When they had heard the king, they departed; and lo, the star, which they saw in the east, went before them, till it came and stood over where the young child was.
>
> When they saw the star, they rejoiced with exceeding great joy.
>
> And when they were come into the house, they saw the young child with Mary his mother, and fell down, and worshiped him; and when they had opened their treasures, they presented unto him gifts; gold, and frankincense, and myrrh.
>
> Matthew 2:1–12

Fortunately for the French people, who dearly loved the custom, a later "real" king, Louis XIV, did not seem to mind a bit. On the contrary, some of the most elaborate Twelfth Night parties were given at Versailles during his reign. On one occasion according to a contemporary account. "The salon had five tables; one for the Princes and Seigneurs, and four for the ladies of the court. . . . At each [a *galette* was served and] a bean discovered inside. At the men's table it fell to the Chief Equerry, who was proclaimed King; at the four other tables it went to a lady of the court. Then the New King and the several New Queens, each in their own little State, chose Ministers, and named Ambassadresses or Ambassadors to make friendly overtures to neighboring Powers, and propose alliances and treaties."

Beans were customarily baked into a Twelfth Night *gâteau*, a yeast cake popular in the South of France, or into a *galette*, a flaky pastry more common in Paris. In any case both became so popular that in the eighteenth century the French *patissiers*, or pastry makers, were moved to ask the government (which regulated such matters) to ban the making of these specialties by their rivals in the guild of bakers. Ironically, after the revolution, these cakes, originally denounced because they were thought to encourage disrespect for the king, were once again denounced, this time because they were associated with the frivolities of the aristocratic *ancien régime*.

Le gros souper (the grand supper) served on Christmas Eve in Provence is a meatless meal although a festive one that ends the long Advent fast. It precedes the midnight Mass. The following dishes are a traditional part of *le gros souper*.

AIOLI

The centerpiece of Le Gros Souper is always a big bowl of *aioli*, the garlic mayonnaise that is the specialty of Provence. The aioli is surrounded by an assortment of vegetables, raw and cooked, and boiled or fried fish fillets. It is a marvelous dish that is perfect for our own buffet or cocktail-party style of entertaining.

For the aioli:

8 cloves garlic
4 egg yolks
Pinch of salt
2¼ cups extra virgin olive oil
Juice of ½ lemon

Pound the garlic in a mortar to a fine paste. Whisk in the egg yolks, one at a time together with the salt. Finally, drizzle in the olive oil, whisking constantly until it is completely absorbed to produce a thick mayonnaise. Whisk in the lemon juice and a little tepid water if the mayonnaise is too thick.

To surround the aioli select from the following:

- *Little new potatoes boiled in their jackets, served warm or room temperature*
- *Carrots, raw and lightly cooked*
- *String beans, briefly steamed or blanched*
- *Artichokes, steamed*
- *Hard-boiled eggs, quartered*
- *Fennel stalks, raw*
- *Celery stalks, raw*
- *Poached fish fillets*
- *Fried fish fillets*

> *Aioli* gently intoxicates, charges the body with warmth, bathes the soul in rapture. In its essence, it concentrates the force and the joy of the sun of Provence. Around an *aioli*, well-perfumed and bright as a vein of gold, where are there men who would not recognize themselves as brothers?
>
> —Frédéric Mistral

TERRINE D'ANGUILLE (BAKED EELS)

Eels are considered a delicacy throughout Europe and are often included in traditional Christmas Eve feasts, which focus on fish and seafood because they are abstinence meals.

4 tablespoons olive oil
3 large leeks, white parts only, cleaned and finely sliced
5 pounds eel, cleaned and skinned
4 cloves garlic, finely chopped
½ cup parsley, finely chopped
½ teaspoon salt
Freshly ground black pepper
2 bay leaves
1 cup black olives (niçoise, if possible), pits removed
1½ cups dry white wine
½ cup bread crumbs

Preheat oven to 350°F.

In a shallow ovenproof casserole large enough to hold the eel, spread 2 tablespoons olive oil and make a bed of the leeks. Mix garlic and parsley together and sprinkle on top of the leeks. Season with salt and pepper and tuck in the bay leaves. Sprinkle with olives and moisten with ½ cup of the white wine. Lay the eel on top of this mixture. Sprinkle the eel with remaining olive oil and bread crumbs. Bake for 1½ hours, basting with white wine until all of it is used up.

Yield: 8 servings.

POMPE À L'HUILE (CHRISTMAS EVE CAKE)

It is traditional to serve thirteen desserts to conclude the Christmas Eve supper. Thirteen, an unlucky number all year long, loses its evil powers on Christmas Eve because of the advent of Christ's powers for good. The thirteen desserts are more symbolic than fancy. They usually include candied fruits, fresh fruits such as oranges, tangerines, apples and pears, chocolates, nougat candies, nuts, dried apricots, and prunes. All these are arranged around special-shaped Christmas Eve cake called *pompe à l'huile.*

3 tablespoons active dry yeast
½ cup warm water (100 to 110°F.)
4½ cups flour, approximately
2 cups brown sugar
Grated rind of 1 lemon
Grated rind of 1 orange
½ teaspoon salt
4 eggs
1 cup best olive oil
2 tablespoons orange-flower water, or 1 tablespoon Grand Marnier

In a small bowl, sprinkle the yeast into the warm water. Stir in ½ cup flour, cover and let stand about 30 minutes, until mixture becomes spongy and doubles in bulk.

Place the remaining flour in a large bowl and stir in the sugar, lemon rind, orange rind, and salt. Beat eggs and olive oil together to just mix and stir into the flour. Add the spongy yeast mixture and mix well to make a soft, smooth dough. Turn out onto lightly floured surface and knead for 8 to 10 minutes.

Put the dough into a oiled bowl and cover with a towel. Let rise for 3 hours. It will double in bulk.

Grease a baking sheet with butter or vegetable shortening.

Punch down and let rise another 3 hours. Punch down and remove to lightly floured surface. Divide the dough into 12 balls and arrange them in a circle, each touching the other, on prepared baking sheet. The circular cake is supposed to vaguely resemble a crown. Cover and let rise for 30 minutes.

Preheat oven to 350°F.

Bake for 35 to 40 minutes, until golden brown. Remove from oven and sprinkle the top of the cake with orange-flower water or Grand Marnier. Let cool before serving.

Yield: 10 to 12 servings.

TURKEY STUFFED WITH PRUNES AND SAUSAGE

Turkey has replaced almost every other bird and beef as the main dish on Christmas Day around the world. This turkey is both roasted and braised and is very moist, juicy, and delicious. It is perfect for a small family Christmas dinner.

1 pound pitted prunes
1 cup hot tea
3 tablespoons cognac
1 pound small breakfast sausages
Liver from the turkey
1 8- to 10-pound turkey
Salt
Freshly ground black pepper
½ cup hot water
1 stick unsalted butter, melted and kept warm

Place the prunes, hot tea, and cognac in a bowl and let steep for at least 1 hour.

Cut the sausages in thirds or quarters and

sauté them in a little butter. Chop the turkey liver roughly and add it for the final 2 or 3 minutes cooking with the sausages.

Preheat oven to 375°F.

Drain the prunes and mix them with the sausages and liver.

Wash and dry the turkey. Sprinkle inside cavity with salt and pepper. Stuff it with the prunes, sausages, and liver. Sew up or skewer the opening. Truss the turkey.

Place the turkey breast side up on a rack in a roasting pan. Brush with melted butter. Roast the turkey for 20 minutes, basting once with more melted butter. Turn the turkey on its side and roast 20 minutes, basting once with melted butter. Turn on other side, roast 20 minutes longer, basting once.

Transfer the turkey to a deep Dutch oven or casserole. Pour ½ cup hot water into the bottom of the roasting pan to deglaze it and pour liquid into Dutch oven or casserole with the turkey. Set cover of Dutch oven on loosely, or cover turkey with aluminum foil. Reduce oven temperature to 325°F. and continue cooking for about 1½ hours, or until juices run clear when the juicy part of turkey is pricked with a fork.

Serve the turkey with pan juices from the bottom of the casserole.

Yield: 6 to 8 servings.

PAIN D'EPICE (SPICE CAKE)

This gingerbread specialty from Dijon is a particular Christmas favorite. Plan ahead and leave several days or a week for the dough to ripen and improve in flavor.

1 cup boiling water
1 cup dark honey
1 cup brown sugar
1 tablespoon baking soda
1 tablespoon anise seeds, crushed
Grated rind of 1 orange
¼ teaspoon salt
1 cup rye flour
3 cups all-purpose flour
½ cup hot milk

Pour the boiling water into a large mixing bowl. Stir in the honey and sugar. Stir in baking soda and mix well to blend. Stir in anise seeds, orange rind, and salt. Sift the flour together and gradually stir it into the liquid mixture. Beat well to make a smooth batter. Cover and let stand in a cool place for several days or even a week.

Preheat oven to 350°F. Grease two 7-inch loaf pans with butter or vegetable shortening.

Divide the batter between the 2 prepared pans. Bake at 350°F. for 1 hour. Remove from oven and brush with hot milk. Cool before serving. This cake keeps well in an airtight container.

Yield: 2 cakes.

BÛCHE DE NOËL (CHRISTMAS LOG)

A famous scrumptious cake baked to resemble and recall to mind the Yule log of ancient days. You can certainly order a *bûche de Noël* from a good bakery but it is not at all difficult to make one at home. *Bûche de Noël* is always served at the *le réveillon*, although it can certainly appear throughout the rest of the Christmas holidays as well. Tradition demands that it must reappear on New Year's Eve with the numbers of the new year displayed an icing on the cake.

The cake:

4 egg yolks
½ teaspoon vanilla extract
1 cup sugar
1 cup all-purpose flour
1 teaspoon baking powder
¼ teaspoon salt
4 egg whites, at room temperature
2–3 tablespoons dark rum
Confectioners' sugar

Mocha Butter Cream:

2 ounces unsweetened chocolate
1¼ cups sugar
½ cup water
4 egg yolks
1 teaspoon vanilla extract
2 teaspoons instant coffee
3 sticks unsalted butter, softened to room temperature
Chocolate for shaving

Preheat oven to 400°F. Grease a 10-by-15-inch jelly-roll pan with butter, line it with waxed paper, and grease the paper with butter.

Preheat oven to 400°F.

Beat the egg yolks and vanilla extract until very light-colored and thick. Gradually beat in the sugar. Sift flour, baking powder, and salt together several times. Fold flour gently into egg-yolk mixture. Beat the egg whites until they form stiff peaks and fold into flour mixture.

Spread the batter evenly in prepared jelly-roll pan. Bake at 400°F. for 12 to 15 minutes, until cake turns light golden brown. Remove from oven and sprinkle with rum. Spread a sheet of waxed paper on the counter and sprinkle the paper with confectioners' sugar. Invert the cake onto the waxed paper and remove the baked-on waxed paper. Use a sharp knife to trim away the crusty edges.

Roll up the cake together with the sugared waxed paper along the long side. Let cool to room temperature for 20 minutes.

Prepare the mocha butter cream: In the top of a double boiler, melt in the chocolate and let it cool.

Combine sugar and water in a saucepan and cook until a candy thermometer registers 238°F. Beat the egg yolks until they are very pale yellow and thick. Then, beating constantly, add the sugar syrup in a slow stream to the egg yolks. Continue beating until the mixture is cool. Stir in the vanilla extract, coffee, and melted chocolate. Gradually beat in the butter. If butter cream seems very soft, cool in refrigerator for 10 to 15 minutes. It should just be of a spreadable consistency.

Unroll the cake and spread half the butter cream on it. Reroll it without the waxed paper, rolling as tightly as possible without breaking it. Chill the cake and the remaining butter cream for several hours. Trim away the edges of the cake, cutting on the diagonal. Cover cake with remaining mocha cream and decorate it with chocolate shavings to look like bark.

Yield: 8 to 10 servings.

CHOCOLATE TRUFFLES

These sophisticated candies are extremely popular in Paris at Christmas time and every other time as well.

6 ounces dark semisweet chocolate
3 tablespoons unsalted butter
2 tablespoons confectioners' sugar
3 egg yolks
1 teaspoon vanilla extract
1 tablespoon dark rum or cognac
½ cup grated semisweet chocolate

In the top of a double boiler, melt the chocolate over boiling water. Whisk in butter and sugar, beating until all the sugar has dissolved. Remove from heat and beat in egg yolks, one at a time, until completely absorbed. Stir in vanilla extract and rum or cognac. Remove to a bowl, cover and let stand overnight in a cool place (but do not refrigerate).

Shape into balls about 1 inch in diameter and roll in grated chocolate. Serve within a day or two as these do not keep well.

Yield: about 2 dozen truffles.

> Finally, the head of the family, the good master, causes to be brought forth, according to his means . . . a cake in which has been hidden a silver coin. He cuts and distributes the cake, keeping back portions for the Infant Jesus, the Virgin and the Magi. These he gives to the poor in their names. Whoever receives the piece containing the coin is recognized as king and all the guests shout for joy.
>
> *Larousse Gastronomique*

GALETTE DES ROIS (CAKE OF KINGS)

A more elaborate version of this traditional Epiphany cake is made with puff pastry, but this simplified version is very pleasing and delicious. The traditional bean has been replaced by a whole almond, eliminating the danger of a broken tooth. The person who finds the almond is king or queen for the next twenty-four hours. At many Parisian parties this means that it is their turn to give the next party and provide another *galette des rois.*

1 cup blanched almonds
2⅓ cups sifted all-purpose flour
¼ teaspoon salt
½ cup sugar
4 egg yolks
1 stick unsalted butter, cut into little pieces
6 to 8 tablespoons ice water
1 whole almond
1 egg yolk mixed with 1 tablespoon water

Place the almonds in the bowl of a food processor and grind them to a fine texture. Add the flour, salt, and sugar and process until well mixed. Add the 4 egg yolks and the butter. Process for a second or two, then with the machine on, add the water one tablespoon at a time until the dough forms a ball. Remove the ball, wrap in plastic, and refrigerate for 1 hour.

Preheat oven to 400°F. Grease a cookie sheet with butter or vegetable shortening.

On a floured surface, roll out the pastry dough into a circle until it is about ¾ inch thick. Press the almonds into the underside of the galette. Trim the edges and place the galette onto the prepared cookie sheet.

Use the point of a sharp knife or knitting needle to decorate the top with swirls and arabesques. Brush the top with egg yolk mixed with water.

Bake at 400°F. for 25 to 30 minutes, or until the cake is golden brown.

Yield: 1 cake.

Christmas in Germany and Austria

Though Christmas is a holiday with profound significance in nearly every part of the Western world, it is safe to say that nowhere is it more elaborately or universally observed than in Germany. Much of the imagery and lore of the Yuletide has its source in the German love of festivity and sentiment.

Many German cities, starting at the very beginning of the Advent season, have a Christ Child's market, a kind of fair of booths and stalls that offer for sale every imaginable kind of Christmas decoration and treat—candles and tinsel and Christmas balls and crib figures, and of course, gingerbread, which is baked especially for Christmas. The fair at Nuremberg, which had its heyday in the eighteenth century, was one of the grandest and oldest in Europe. It featured hundreds of booths and stalls and there was always a child dressed as an angel to welcome visitors. Among the wares offered there were the traditional Lebkuchen, or honey cakes, as well as small figures of the infant Jesus, which were given as symbolic presents.

The Advent season includes the four Sundays preceding Christmas and ends on Christmas Day. In Germany a greenery wreath is customarily set out with four purple candles, one to be lit each Sunday, and a large white candle in the center to be lit on Christmas Day. Special Advent calendars, elaborately decorated and often featuring cut-out windows to be opened on particular days, were made for the children, and like many other German Christmas customs, this one has spread throughout much of the world.

December 24 being the feast day of Adam and Eve, it was the custom in Germany during the Middle Ages to put on mystery plays that enacted the events of their lives. An unvarying feature of the plays was a decorated evergreen tree representing the Tree of Life from which they ate and so

caused the fall of man. Over the centuries the plays, along with the festivities associated with them, strayed somewhat from their religious origins, and the Church felt moved to abandon sponsoring them. Nevertheless, the people continued to set up and decorate trees in their homes, and thus the tradition of the Christmas tree is said to have been born in Germany. Nowhere else in the world is as much trouble and care taken with the decoration of Christmas trees as in Germany. In fact, it was in Thuringia around 1880 that glassmakers discovered how to make the blown glass balls, bells, and other ornaments that today are almost universally used to make the Christmas tree festive.

As in most European countries, it is St. Nicholas who brings gifts to German children on the eve of his feast day, December 6—but he does not come alone. His companion is usually of dark complexion and generally less jolly than Nicholas himself (if not out-and-out frightening). In southern Germany and Austria the companion is known as Krampus, in the northwest as Pelzebock or Pelznickel, in the Rhineland as Hans Muff, in Silesia as Bartel, in Hesse as Gumphinkel. Since the Reformation, however, in many areas he has been most commonly called Knecht Ruprecht. He carries a bundle of switches, as a reminder to children to be good throughout the year.

After the Reformation, the authorities increasingly frowned upon the idea of having Nicholas dressed up as a bishop and distributing gifts, and Santa Claus, in his more modern (and secular) incarnation became increasingly popular: the familiar friendly old man with long white beard, fur-trimmed hood, and sleigh. Some confusion about his name still remains, and in various outlying parts of Germany he is known variously as Klaasbuur, Burklaas, Rauklas, Bullerklaas, and Sunnerklas. The farther east you go in Germany the more the gift giver figure retains his connection with the pagan past. In Pomerania they call him "Ash Man," in West Prussia "Shaggy Goat," and on the East Prussian plains they call him "Rider." In modern times in Germany as elsewhere in the world, he has been increasingly transformed into Father Christmas, a Santa Claus figure who appears not on the eve of St. Nicholas's feast day, but on Christmas Eve.

Weihnachten

For many Germans, the highpoint of the holiday celebrations is the Christmas Mass, held in recent times by both Protestant and Catholic churches at midnight on Christmas Eve, although until recently Catholic services were held at six Christmas morning. This has given rise to many romantic depictions of throngs of churchgoers wending their way to a rustic church, each carrying a candle or lantern to light the way through the dark and snowy landscape.

One of the most famous of all Christmas songs, "Silent Night! Holy Night!," was written in 1818 in a small town called Oberndorf near Salzburg. The assistant priest, Joseph Mohr, wanted a new song for the Christmas festival and gave some lines he had written to the organist, Frances Xaver Gruber, just a few hours before services were to commence. Though for many years the authors of the song were completely forgotten, the song was not. Since that time it has been translated into 44 languages and remains perhaps the most widely known and best loved Christmas song in the world.

Rumtopf (Rum Pot—Summer Fruits Preserved in Rum)

Here is a German Christmas specialty that must be prepared at the height of summer. For the fruit, use any of the suggested soft fruits, and others you think of.

Strawberries, blueberries, raspberries, blackberries, pitted cherries, apricots, peaches, plums
1 pound sugar for every 2 pounds fruit
Dark rum or Brandy

Choose a large glass or ceramic crock that will fit into a corner of the refrigerator. As fruits come into season, wash and dry them. Remove any pits. Mix with sugar and place into the crock. Add rum to cover. Add more fruit, sugar, and rum as the summer goes on.

Serve at Christmastime over ice cream, custard, or cake.

Christstollen (Christmas Bread)

This sweet Christmas bread has been a specialty of Dresden at Christmastime since the Middle Ages. The bread is very rich and filled with dried fruits and nuts. It keeps extremely well and makes a lovely gift all on its own.

2 cups milk
1 cup sugar
1 teaspoon salt
2 sticks unsalted butter
2 packages active dry yeast
¼ cup warm water
8 cups flour
4 eggs, well beaten
2 teaspoons vanilla extract
1½ cups golden raisins
1½ cups blanched almonds, roughly chopped
½ cup currants
½ cup citron, chopped
1 tablespoon candied orange peel, chopped
Grated rind of lemon
1 stick unsalted butter, melted
½ cup sugar
Cinnamon

Heat the milk in a saucepan until almost boiling and remove from heat. In a large mixing bowl, combine the scalded milk with the sugar, salt and butter. Stir until all the butter has melted and let cool to lukewarm.

Sprinkle the yeast along with a pinch of sugar into the warm water. Let stand for 5 to 10 minutes until frothy. Stir the yeast mixture into the milk and stir in 2 cups of the flour. Stir well to make a smooth batter. Let stand in a warm place until very bubbly, about 30 minutes.

Stir in the beaten eggs, the vanilla extract and the remaining 6 cups flour, to make a soft but workable dough. Mix together the raisins, almonds, currants, citron, candied orange peel and lemon rind.

Remove dough to a lightly floured surface and knead in the fruit and nut mixture. Continue to knead the dough until it is smooth and elastic, about 10 minutes.

Place the dough in a greased bowl, cover and let rest in a warm place until double in bulk, 1½ to 2 hours. Punch down dough and knead lightly for about 5 minutes and divide the dough into three equal parts. Let rest for 15 minutes.

Flatten each piece of dough into an oval shape and roll out until it is approximately ¾ inch thick, brush with melted butter and sprinkle with sugar and cinnamon. Fold each oval, one long side over so that it extends a little past the center of the oval. Press down gently but firmly.

Arrange the stollen fold side up on lightly greased baking sheets. Brush with melted butter, cover loosely with a towel, and let rise until double in bulk, about 1 hour.

Preheat oven to 425°F.

Bake at 425°F. for 10 minutes, reduce oven temperature to 350°F. and bake for 40 minutes longer. Remove from oven and let cool. Glaze with white Sugar Icing, page 115 and decorate with large pieces of glacé fruit and nuts.

Yield: 3 stollen.

ROAST GOOSE

Giblets from the goose
2 medium onions
1 stalk celery with leaves
1 bay leaf
1 tablespoon dried salt
Freshly ground black pepper
1 8-pound goose
1 tablespoon dried marjoram
6 cloves
2 apples
1 cup orange juice
2 tablespoons cornstarch
¼ cup cold water

In a saucepan combine the giblets with 1 onion, the celery stalk (broken into 3 pieces), bay leaf, salt, and freshly ground black pepper. Cover with 3 cups water and simmer for 1 hour. Strain and reserve the stock.

Wash and dry the goose. Sprinkle the inside cavity with marjoram. Stick cloves into the second onion and place onion in cavity together with the apples. Sew or skewer the opening together.

Preheat oven to 400° F.

Place the goose on a rack in a roasting pan breast side down. Roast for 45 minutes, then drain fat from the pan. Reduce oven temperature to 350 ° F. and roast 1 hour longer. Turn goose breast side up, and cook until golden brown—30 minutes. Remove from oven and let rest for 20 minutes. Pour off most of the fat from the roasting pan. Add 1 cup of stock and the orange juice to deglaze the pan. Scrape up all the browned bits from the bottom of the pan. Mix cornstarch with water and add to the pan. Cook over medium heat, stirring constantly until gravy is thickened.

Serve with Braised Sweet and Sour Cabbage (following recipe).

Yield: 6 servings.

Braised Sweet and Sour Cabbage

This dish is even better made a day ahead.

3 tablespoons bacon fat or vegetable oil
2 medium onions, sliced thin
1 head red cabbage, sliced thin
1 cup raisins
½ cup red currant jelly
1 bay leaf
½ teaspoon salt
Freshly ground black pepper
2 tablespoons red wine vinegar

Heat the bacon fat in a large skillet or sauté pan. Sauté the onions until wilted, about 15 minutes. Add the cabbage and sauté, stirring frequently, until wilted, about 10 minutes. Add the raisins, red currant jelly, bay leaf, salt, and freshly ground black pepper to taste. Stir in ¼ cup water, cover, and simmer for about 1 hour, until very tender. Stir in vinegar and adjust seasonings.

Yield: 6 servings.

Christmas in Greece

St. Nicholas is the patron saint of sailors, and Greece, with its long shoreline and myriad islands, is a nation of sailors, so it is not surprising that the Greek people are particularly devoted to him. Yet for Greek Christians as for most followers of the Eastern Orthodox Church, Christmas definitely takes second place to Easter in the ranking of holidays. Christmas trees, for instance, are rare in Greece, and gift giving is generally done on St. Basil's Day (January 1). Nevertheless, there are many customs and traditions associated with the Christmas season in Greece.

Early Christmas morning Greek children go from house to house offering traditional songs and good wishes to the members of each household where they stop. Often they are rewarded with gifts of dried figs, walnuts, almonds, or other sweets. In England the songs would be called carols; in Greece they are known as *kalanda*.

Pigs, fattened since summer, are traditionally slaughtered and eaten for the Christmas feast, and on nearly every table there is *christopsomo* ("Christ bread") for the holiday. The bread, made in large sweet loaves, varies in shape, but the crust is customarily engraved and ornamented in some way that reflects the family's profession.

On St. Basil's Day all the pitchers and water jugs in the house must be emptied and refilled with new "St Basil's water." This ceremony of the "renewal of waters" is often accompanied by offerings to the naiads or spirits that live in springs and fountains. As with the Scottish custom of the "first footing," the people of Greece are often quite particular about the choice of who will first set foot in a home on New Year's Day, though the luckiest choice is hardly ever a stranger, but rather the master of the house,

or some specially chosen family member. This is also a time when it is traditional to break a pomegranate on the threshold.

There are a number of widespread beliefs concerning the *Kallikantzaroi*, a race of ogrelike creatures thought to live below the earth but who walk abroad during the twelve days between Christmas and Epiphany. More mischievous than actually evil, they are thought to extinguish fires, sour the milk, spoil cakes, and braid the tails of horses together. Elaborate rituals harking back to the very earliest Greek cultures are performed to protect one's home and person from these demons. In coastal villages, a priest throws a small cross into the water on Epiphany, which is supposed to drive the Kallikantzaroi back to their below-ground haunts for the rest of the year, and young boys dive to retrieve it. Homes, too, are sprinkled with holy water to be sure that no evil lingers behind.

Preparing for Christmas involves forty days of fasting to purify the soul through prayer and penitence. Baking is done the last week before Christmas.

KOURABIEDES (SHORTBREAD)

These delicious cookies are served in every Greek home at Christmas and on many other festive occasions. But at Christmastime they are usually studded with cloves to commemorate the Magi, who brought spices to the Christ Child.

4 sticks unsalted butter, at room temperature
3/4 cup confectioners' sugar
1 egg yolk
2 tablespoons brandy or cognac
4 1/2 cups sifted all-purpose flour
About 72 whole cloves
Confectioners' sugar for topping

Preheat oven to 350°F.

Cream the butter until it is very fluffy. Gradually beat in sugar. Beat in the egg yolk and brandy or cognac. Gradually blend in flour to make a soft dough. Shape the dough with floured hands into balls the size of a walnut. Stud each ball with 1 whole clove. Arrange the cookies on an ungreased baking sheet. Bake for 15 minutes until a very pale sand color. Do not let them get brown. Cool on wire racks and sift confectioners' sugar over the cookies before storing in an airtight container.

Yield: 5 to 6 dozen cookies.

DIPLES

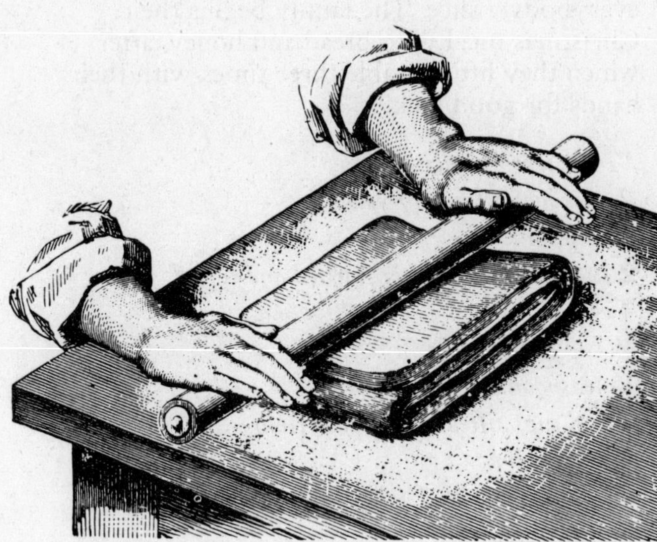

In Greek, *diples* means "folds," and the shape of these cookies refers to the Christ Child's diapers or swaddling clothes. They are a kind of deep-fried cruller served with honey syrup and they are yummy.

5 eggs
½ cup sugar
½ cup olive oil
Grated rind of 1 orange
3½ cups flour
Pinch of salt
1 teaspoon baking powder
3 to 4 cups vegetable oil for deep frying
½ cup honey
½ cup water
1 teaspoon cinnamon
1 tablespoon lemon juice
⅔ cup chopped pistachio nuts
Confectioners' sugar

Beat the eggs together with the sugar until very light and fluffy. Beat in olive oil and orange rind. Sift together the flour, salt, and baking powder and stir gradually into the egg and sugar mixture. Remove the dough to a lightly floured surface and knead for 10 minutes, until the dough is smooth and elastic. Cover and let rest for 20 minutes.

Roll the dough out very thin and use a pastry cutter to cut out 1½-inch squares. Fold into triangles and join the ends to make "diapers." Be sure to press the corners well so that the diapers don't come undone.

In a heavy kettle heat the vegetable oil until it registers 370°F. on a deep-frying thermometer. Drop the diples a few at a time into the hot fat and fry for about 4 minutes, turning them over once, until golden brown on both sides. Drain on paper towels. Continue until all are done.

In a saucepan combine honey, water, cinnamon, and lemon juice. Bring to a boil, reduce heat and simmer for 1 minute.

Dribble the honey syrup over the fried diples, sprinkle with chopped pistachio nuts and confectioners' sugar.

Yield: about 4 dozen.

Christmas Husbandly Fare

Good husband and huswife, now chiefly be glad,
things handsome to have, as they ought to be had.
They both do provide, against Christmas do come,
to welcome their neighbors, good chere to have some.

Good bread and good drinke, a good fier in the hall,
brawne, pudding, and souse, and good mustard withal.
Biefe, mutton, and Porke, and good Pies of the best,
pig, veale, goose, and capon, and turkey wel drest,
Chese, apples, and nuttes, and good Caroles to heare,
as then, in the countrey is counted good cheare.

What cost to good husbande, is any of this?
good household provision onely it is:
Of other the like, I do leave out a meny,
that costeth the husband never a peny.

Thomas Tusser (1573)

CHRISTOPSOMO (CHRIST BREAD)

On Christmas Eve every housewife bakes a christopsomo, literally "Christ bread." It is a sweet bread and is made in large loaves of various shapes, with ornaments engraved on the crust. The Christmas table is ceremoniously laid on the eve of the great day. The housewife lays out the Christmas bread and a pot of honey. Around these she scatters various dried fruits and nuts. The master of the house then makes the sign of the cross over the loaf with his knife; he wishes everyone a happy Christmas—*"chronia polla"*—cuts the loaf, and gives everybody a slice. The family begins their Christmas meal with bread and honey, after which they lift the table three times with their hands for good luck.

½ cup warm water
2 packages active dry yeast
½ cup milk
2 sticks unsalted butter, melted and cooled
4 eggs
¾ cup sugar
¼ teaspoon salt
7 to 8 cups sifted all-purpose flour
walnut halves
1 egg beaten with 1 tablespoon water
Sesame seeds

Sprinkle the yeast into the warm water along with a pinch of sugar. Let stand 5 to 10 minutes, until dissolved.

Stir the milk into the yeast mixture. Stir in the melted butter and beat in the eggs. Stir in sugar and salt. Gradually stir in flour, enough to make a workable dough. Remove to a lightly floured surface and knead for 10 minutes until the dough is smooth and elastic. Place the dough in a greased bowl, cover, and let stand in a warm place until double in bulk, 1½ to 2 hours.

Punch down and knead briefly, about 5 minutes. Remove a small piece of dough and reserve. Shape the bread into a large round loaf and place on a lightly greased baking sheet or in a round cake pan. Work the small piece of dough into the shape of a cross and place on top of the loaf. Press walnut halves along the edges of the cross. Cover the bread loosely with a towel and let rise in a warm place until double in bulk, about 1½ hours.

Preheat oven to 350°F.

Brush the top of the bread with beaten egg and sprinkle with sesame seeds. Bake about 45 minutes, until bread is golden brown and sounds hollow when tapped.

Let cool before serving.

Yield: 1 loaf.

VASILOPITA

This New Year's bread is named after St. Basil ("Vassily" in Greek), the patron saint of the New Year. Traditionally it is served on the stroke of midnight, New Year's Eve, and like many other holiday cakes has a silver coin hidden inside. The bread is first blessed, then the head of the household cuts the first slice and it is reserved for and dedicated to Christ. The second slice is for the Virgin Mary, and the third for St. Basil. Whoever finds the coin has a special blessing from St. Basil for the coming year. The reserved pieces of bread and any leftovers after the family is served are distributed to the poor.

½ cup milk
1 cup sugar
½ teaspoon salt
2 sticks unsalted butter, melted and cooled
¼ cup lukewarm water
2 packages active dry yeast
1 tablespoon sugar
3 eggs
6 to 6½ cups sifted all-purpose flour
2 tablespoons melted butter
1 egg, beaten with 1 tablespoon water
½ cup blanched slivered almonds

In a saucepan bring the milk to a boil and remove from heat immediately. Stir in sugar, salt, and melted butter. Let cool to lukewarm.

In a large mixing bowl, combine ¼ cup lukewarm water, yeast, and 1 tablespoon sugar. Let stand until yeast has dissolved, 5 to 10 minutes. Stir the lukewarm milk mixture into the yeast. Beat the eggs and stir into the milk-yeast mixture. Gradually stir in 3 cups of flour and beat until smooth. Stir in additional flour to make a dough. When stiff enough to handle remove it to a lightly floured surface and knead for about 10 minutes until dough is smooth and elastic. Place the dough in a greased bowl and brush the top with melted butter. Cover and let stand in a warm place until doubled in bulk, 1½ to 2 hours.

Grease a large baking sheet with butter or vegetable shortening.

Punch down the dough and knead briefly, about 5 minutes. Shape the dough into one large round loaf or two smaller ones. Insert a silver coin in the bread dough. Arrange the loaf or loaves on prepared baking sheets, cover loosely with a towel, and let rise until doubled in bulk, about 1 hour.

Preheat oven to 375°F.

Brush the top of bread or breads with the beaten egg and decorate with slivered almonds. Bake for 45 to 60 minutes. Two smaller loaves will be done sooner than one large one. The bread is done when it is golden brown on the outside, and sounds hollow when tapped on the bottom.

Yield: 1 large or 2 small loaves of bread.

CHRISTMAS IN ITALY

If the Christmas tree owes its popularity to Germany, then to Italy goes the distinction of introducing the Christmas crib or Nativity scene. It was in fact at the specific request of St. Francis of Assisi that in the village of Greccio a man named Giovanni Vellita prepared the first such likeness of a manger. St. Francis celebrated the Mass before it, inspiring such awe and devotion in the hearts of those who came that the Nativity scene remains today one of the most enduring symbols of the holiday season.

St. Francis also paved the way for the development of an amazingly rich folk art tradition—the making of crib figures or *pastori*. In eighteenth-century Naples the Bourbon king, Carlo II, developed a virtual mania for creating elaborate tableaux, and his enthusiasm quickly spread to all the upper classes. At the same time, through the efforts of a Dominican friar named Gregorio Maria Rocco, the common people were encouraged to build their own Nativity scenes. The idea soon spread all over Italy and from there to France and indeed to the rest of the world.

On Christmas Eve, cannon are fired at the Castel St. Angelo in Rome to proclaim the beginning of the holiday season, and a strict twenty-four-hour fast is ended with an elaborate Christmas feast, after which small presents are drawn, grab-bag style, from the Urn of Fate.

Serious gift giving, however, generally waits until the feast of the Epiphany, a very important part of the holiday season in Italy. According to Italian legend, the three wise men paused in their travels to ask an old woman for shelter and nourishment. She refused them, and they travelled on; within a few hours she had a change of heart—but by them the Magi were long gone. The old woman, now known as La Befana, meaning Epiphany, still searches for the Christ Child and is depicted in many ways, as a fairy queen, a crone, even a witch. She visits Italian homes each Epiphany, bringing both gifts for good children and the threat of punishment for the others. On the eve of the Epiphany, a bell is tolled to warn children that they must hurry off to bed before La Befana arrives.

In many regions of Italy Christmas Eve dinner is the most exciting meal of the year, despite the fact Christmas Eve is still a fast day and the eating of meat is prohibited. Fish, then, has a starring role, and the Italians do it splendid justice. In Sicily, a twenty-four-hour fast precedes *il cenone*, the Christmas Eve dinner, which may include as many as twenty different fish dishes. In many homes it is traditional to serve seven different fish cooked seven different ways, representing the seven sacraments. Although you may not want to cook all seven of the following dishes for one meal, each one makes a festive entrée for a Christmas Eve dinner.

Anguille in Umido al Vino Bianco (Stewed Eel)

2 pounds of eels, skinned and cleaned at the fish shop
½ cup olive oil
1 medium onion,thinly sliced
1 clove garlic, peeled and smashed
1 cup canned Italian tomatoes, roughly chopped
1 cup dry white wine
2 sage leaves or ½ teaspoon dried sage
1 teaspoon grated lemon peel
¼ cup parsley, chopped
Salt
Freshly ground black pepper

Cut the eels into 2-inch pieces. In a large frying pan, heat the olive oil and sauté the onions and garlic for 10 minutes, until just translucent. Add the eels and sauté for 15 minutes. Add tomatoes, white wine, sage, lemon peel, parsley, salt, and freshly ground black pepper to taste. Cover and simmer gently for 30 minutes.
Yield: 6 servings.

Vongole Oreganate (Stuffed Baked Clams)

36 littleneck clams
½ cup dry white wine
1½ cups bread crumbs
⅔ cup freshly grated Parmesan cheese
¼ cup flat-leafed Italian parsley, finely chopped
2 teaspoons finely chopped garlic
1 teaspoon oregano
Freshly ground black pepper
½ cup olive oil
2 lemons, cut in wedges

Scrub the clams under cold running water and place them in a large pot with the white wine. Cover the pot and cook over medium heat for 10 to 15 minutes, until clams open. Remove from heat and remove opened clams to a large bowl. Strain the broth through several layers of cheesecloth or through a paper coffee filter and reserve.

In a mixing bowl combine the bread crumbs, Parmesan cheese, parsley, garlic, oregano, and black pepper to taste. Add 2 tablespoons of the olive oil and enough of the strained clam broth to make a mixture that is moist throughout.

Discard top half of each clam shell and arrange clams on the half shell on a large baking sheet. Cover each clam with some of the bread-crumb stuffing. Drizzle remaining olive oil over the clams. Place under broiler for 10 to 12 minutes, until the stuffing is brown and crusty.

Serve with lemon wedges.
Yield: Six servings.

RISOTTO CON FRUTTI DI MARE (RICE WITH SHELLFISH)

This is not cooked like a traditional risotto, so you can use regular long-grain rice. Because you don't have to stir it for twenty minutes it means less work, but the result is still a delicious dish quite suitable to serve at the Christmas Eve table.

4 tablespoons olive oil
1 clove garlic, finely minced
½ teaspoon red pepper flakes
1 pound shrimp, cleaned and deveined
1 pound mussels
1 pound littleneck clams
1 cup dry white wine
2 cups long-grain rice
¼ cup flat-leafed Italian parsley, chopped
Salt
Freshly ground black pepper

In a large skillet or saucepan, heat 2 tablespoons of the olive oil and sauté the the garlic for 5 minutes but do not brown. Add the red pepper flakes and the shrimp and cook for two minutes until the shrimp start to turn pink. Remove from the heat and reserve.

Scrub and clean the clams and mussels. Put them in a large pot together with the remaining olive oil and the white wine. Cover and bring to a boil. Cook for about 10 minutes until the shellfish have opened. Remove the opened shellfish to a large bowl, discarding any that have not opened. Strain the cooking liquid through several layers of cheesecloth or a paper coffee filter. Measure the strained liquid. Remove shellfish from their shells and add to the shrimp. Strain any juices that have accumulated in the bottom of the bowl and add to the shellfish.

Add enough water to the strained cooking liquid to measure 4 cups. Put the liquid in a heavy pot together with the rice and bring to a boil. Stir, cover, and reduce heat to a simmer. Cook about 10 minutes, remove the lid and add the shellfish and all the sauce. Add the parsley. Stir well and cook uncovered, stirring frequently until the rice has absorbed all the liquid and is tender.

Yield: 6 to 8 servings.

SPAGHETTINI WITH TUNA AND ANCHOVIES

This dish is delicious, quick, and easy and nothing says you have to wait until Christmas Eve to try it. It is also the perfect, soothing conclusion after a hard day of Christmas shopping.

2 tablespoons unsalted butter
16½-ounce can Italian-style tuna packed in olive oil
Freshly ground black pepper
12-ounce can anchovies, drained
1 tablespoon capers
3 tablespoons parsley, finely chopped
1 pound spaghettini

Set 5 to 6 quarts water to boil in a large pot.

In a large saucepan, melt the butter and stir in the tuna, breaking it up with a fork. Add freshly ground black pepper to taste (a lot is good here), the anchovies, and capers. Simmer over low heat for 10 minutes. Stir in parsley and turn off heat.

Cook spaghettini al dente. Drain and add it to the sauce in the saucepan. Toss well and serve in warmed bowls.
Yield: 4 to 6 servings.

ZUPPA DI COZZE (MUSSEL SOUP)

4 pounds fresh mussels
4 tablespoons olive oil
3 cloves garlic, smashed and peeled
1 cup dry white wine
2 cups water
2 tablespoons unsalted butter
1 medium onion, finely chopped
2 stalks celery, finely chopped
1½ cups canned Italian tomatoes, chopped with their liquid
¼ cup flat-leafed parsley, finely chopped
1 teaspoon oregano
2 cups fish stock or clam broth
Freshly ground black pepper

Scrub the mussels with a hard-bristled brush under cold running water and remove the "beards" by pulling them out. Soak the scrubbed mussels in cold water for 30 minutes.

In a large saucepan combine the mussels, olive oil, garlic, white wine, and water. Cover and bring to a boil. Cook for 10 to 15 minutes, or until mussels have opened. Remove from heat and remove sand. Reserve all the liquid.

In a heavy saucepan, melt the butter and sauté the onion and celery for about 15 to 20 minutes, until the onion starts to turn golden. Add the tomatoes, parsley, oregano, and fish stock or clam broth. Add the reserved liquid from the mussels. Simmer gently for 10 to 15 minutes, then add the mussels (in their shells) and cook for a few minutes to heat through. Season with freshly ground black pepper to taste.

Serve in deep soup bowls with crusty Italian bread.
Yield: 6 servings

FRITTO MISTO DI PESCI

This mixed fish fry is very much a traditional Christmas Eve dish and is often served on its own with some vegetables tossed into the batter and fried as well. If you would like to include vegetables, consider zucchini, mushrooms, eggplant, broccoli, and artichokes.

1½ cups all-purpose flour
½ teaspoon salt
3 tablespoons olive oil
2 eggs, separated
1 cup water
3 to 4 cups vegetable oil for frying
1 pound small squid, cleaned at fish market
1 pound halibut
1 pound whitefish
½ pound shrimp (or substitute same amount of any other fish or your choice)
2 lemons, cut into wedges

In a large bowl, mix the flour with salt and stir in olive oil, egg yolks, and water to make a batter. Cover and let stand for 1 hour. Beat the egg whites until they form stiff peaks and fold into batter.

Cut the squid into ½-inch strips. Wash and dry the fish and cut into bite-size pieces. Shell and devein the shrimp.

In a deep heavy straight-sided kettle, heat the oil until it registers 370°F. on a deep-frying thermometer.

Dip fish in batter and fry a few at a time until golden on both sides. Do not overcrowd in the frying pot. Remove with slotted spoon and drain on paper towels.

Arrange on large platter and surround with lemon wedges.
Yield: 6 to 8 servings.

ORANGE AND ONION SALAD

This lovely salad is a Sicilian Christmas Eve specialty.

4 to 6 navel oranges
1 large red onion
10 leaves of romaine lettuce
½ teaspoon salt
Freshly ground black-pepper
¼ cup extra virgin olive oil

With a sharp paring knife, cut away the skin and membrane from the oranges. Cut horizontally into circles about ½-inch thick. Peel the onion and slice into very thin rings. Arrange lettuce leaves on a large platter or in a shallow bowl. Arrange overlapping layers of orange slices and onion slices. Sprinkle with salt and pepper and drizzle with olive oil.
Yield: 8 to 10 servings.

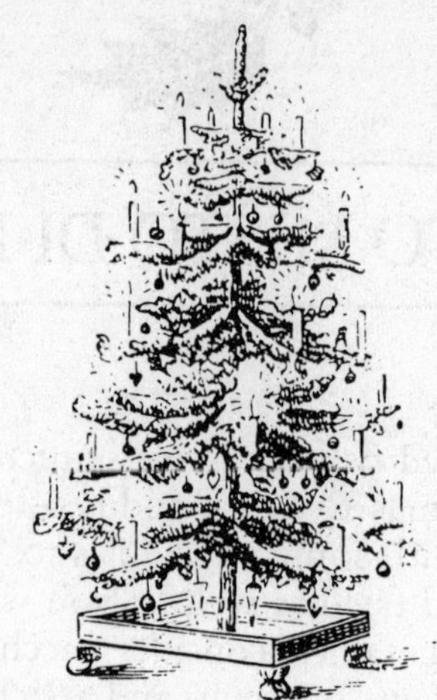

BACCALA ALLA ROMANA (CODFISH ROMAN STYLE)

Dried salted cod is a Christmas favorite in many European countries. This Roman specialty piquant with tomatoes and raisins is particularly delicious.

2 pounds dried cod
3 large onions, thinly sliced
3 tablespoons olive oil
3 cups canned Italian tomatoes, roughly chopped
1 teaspoon freshly ground pepper
4 tablespoons white raisins
Salt

Soak the cod for 12 to 24 hours in cold water to cover. Change the water several times during the soaking.

In a large skillet or saucepan, sauté the onions in the olive oil for 20 to 30 minutes, until the onions are soft and turning gold. Add the tomatoes and pepper. Simmer gently for 20 minutes.

Cut the cod into 2-inch chunks and add to the sauce. Add the raisins and cook over low heat for about 15 minutes until the fish begins to flake. Taste for salt.

Serve with hot crusty Italian bread.
Yield: 6 to 8 servings.

PANETTONE (ITALIAN CHRISTMAS BREAD)

This lovely bread becomes Easter bread in the spring and pops up for other festive occasions, and no wonder, for it is truly delectable.

2 packages dry yeast
½ cup warm milk
⅔ cup sugar
6 eggs
½ teaspoon salt
1 pound butter, melted
6 cups all-purpose flour
1 cup golden raisins
½ cup citron, roughly chopped
1 tablespoon grated lemon rind
2 tablespoons melted butter
½ cup confectioners' sugar

In a bowl, sprinkle the yeast in the milk and let stand to dissolve. Add sugar and mix well. Beat in eggs, one at a time, to blend. Stir in salt and melted butter. Gradually stir in the flour to make a dough. Remove dough to a lightly floured surface and knead for 10 to 15 minutes until dough is smooth and elastic. Put the dough in a greased bowl, cover and set aside to rise in a warm place. Let rise until double in bulk, about 1½ hours.

Grease two 8-inch round cake pans with butter

Punch down dough and remove to a lightly floured surface. Knead in raisins, citron and lemon rind. Knead for about 10 minutes. Divide dough in half and shape into balls. Place each into prepared cake pan. Cover and let dough rise until double in bulk, about 1 hour.

Preheat oven to 350°F.

With a small, sharp knife, cut a cross in the top of each bread. Bake for 30 to 40 minutes, until the crust is golden brown. Brush the tops with melted butter and sprinkle with confectioners' sugar.

Serve warm, cold, or toasted with butter. Yield: 2 breads.

Christmas in Mexico

The Spanish word *posada* means "inn" or "hostel" and in Mexico at Christmastime *las posadas* refers to the religious processions that reenact Joseph and Mary's frustrated search for lodgings in Bethlehem. The processions start nine days before Christmas (since the original journey from Nazareth took nine days), and are put on by friends or family members who divide themselves into two groups: pilgrims and innkeepers.

The pilgrims travel from house to house, or from room to room within one house, and at each door they ask for shelter and at each they are ritually refused, until they finally reach the door of a room where an altar has been set up, including a Nativity scene complete with houses, sheep, and sheperds, and of course figures of the Holy Family. The pilgrims are admitted and then this traditional prayer is spoken:

> O God, who in coming to save us, did not disdain
> humble stable, grant that we may never close our hearts
> when thou art knocking so that we may be made worthy to
> be received into thy sight when our hour comes.

After food and drink are served, it is time for the piñata party. The piñata, an earthenware jar made in the imaginative shape of animals, ships, houses or people, and filled with small presents or treats, is suspended from the branch of a tree, and the children are blindfolded and each in turn is given a chance to try and break open the piñata with a large stick. When at last one of the children is successful, there is a mad scramble to gather up the treats that have showered down upon them.

Another Christmas tradition in Mexico are the *puestos,* elaborately decorated market stalls that are set up weeks before Christmas in the plazas of every town and city by the Indians, many of whom travel for days from their homes in the more remote areas. Here every conceivable kind of craft is offered—pottery, carvings, paintings, etc. and an endless variety of foodstuffs, including cheeses, bananas, candies, cookies, figs, dates, peppers, nuts, and always orchids, poinsettias, and dozens of other varieties of flowers.

It is believed that the seventeenth-century Mexican Franciscans were the first to include poinsettias in the Christmas celebration. Dr. Joel Poinsett, the first foreign minister from the United States to Mexico, sent cuttings of the poinsettia to friends up north, and it is for him that the flower is named.

The poinsettia, especially, is considered "the flower of Christmas Eve." There is a story that a little boy named Pablo was on his way to visit the manger at the church in his village; having no offering to make, he gathered up some unadorned green branches that grew along the road. The other children made fun of him, but when he laid the poinsettia branches by the manger, each branch was graced with a brilliant red star-shaped flower.

ENSALADA DE NOCHEBUENA (CHRISTMAS EVE SALAD)

This meatless salad is a traditional part of the Christmas Eve dinner in Mexico.

¾ cup olive oil
3 tablespoons orange juice
2 tablespoons red wine vinegar
1 teaspoon salt
1 tablespoon fresh coriander, chopped (optional)
1 head romaine lettuce
2 beets, cooked and julienned
2 apples, peeled and sliced in thin wedges
2 oranges, peeled and sliced into thin rounds
2 bananas, sliced into rounds
1 cup pineapple cubes (fresh or canned)
½ cup unsalted peanuts
1 pomegranate (optional)

In a small bowl whisk together the olive oil, red-wine vinegar, salt, and fresh coriander if using. Set aside. Wash and dry the leaves of the romaine lettuce. Shred the lettuce leaves. Arrange the shredded lettuce on a large platter or in the bottom of a large glass bowl. Arrange the other ingredients (except peanuts and pomegranate) in layers. Toss together gently with the reserved dressing. Top the salad with peanuts and the seeds of the pomegranate.

Yield: 6 to 8 servings.

Images of the three kings and their gifts are unvarying elements in Nativity scenes and other Christmas decorations, though of course they are more properly associated with the Epiphany, the eve of which is known as Twelfth Night. As most children know (and most adults tend to forget), the three kings were Melchior, king of Arabia and the bearer of gold; Balthazar, king of Ethiopia and bearer of frankincense; and Caspar, king of Tarsus, who brought myrrh. Thus they were indeed three kings, but they are also referred to as Magi (singular Magus) which in this context means that they were priests of the Zoroastrian religion, and as such would have been adept at astrology and other forms of divination.

Bunuelos

At Christmastime there is no bigger treat in Mexico than a crispy fried *bunuelo* sitting in a sweet puddle of cinnamon-flavored syrup. Sometimes bunuelos are served on inexpensive pottery plates that are hurled to the ground and smashed after the delicious doughnut has been consumed. This extravagant gesture is said to bring good luck in the coming year. In any case, it sure is fun!

4 cups all-purpose flour
2 tablespoons sugar
1 teaspoon baking powder
½ teaspoon salt
1 cup milk
1 large egg
1 teaspoon anise seeds, crushed

3 to 4 cups vegetable oil for frying

Sift the flour, sugar, baking powder, and salt into large bowl. In another bowl, whisk the milk and egg together until frothy. Stir the anise seeds into the milk and stir the milk mixture into the flour to make a dough.

Remove dough to a lightly floured surface and knead lightly until it is smooth and satiny, 5 to 10 minutes. Divide the dough into approximately 30 pieces and shape them into balls. Cover with a cloth and let stand for 20 minutes.

On a lightly floured surface, roll each ball out into a circle about the size of a tortilla.

In a heavy, deep kettle, heat the oil to 360°F. Fry bunuelos a few at a time for 3 to 5 minutes, turning once, until they are golden brown and puffy. Drain on paper towels. Serve warm with Cinnamon-Wine Sauce.

Cinnamon-Wine Sauce

¾ cup dry red wine
⅓ cup brown sugar
½ cup raisins
½ teaspoon cinnamon

In a medium saucepan, heat the wine, sugar, raisins, and cinnamon. Simmer, stirring, until sugar is completely dissolved. Spoon the syrup over freshly fried bunuelos.

Christmas in Central and Eastern Europe

Czechoslovakia, whose western half was once known as Bohemia, was the home of Good King Wenceslaus, way back in the tenth century. English troops fighting in Bohemia hundreds of years later are said to have brought home the hymn that sings the praises of this early convert to Christianity.

St. Nicholas (called in Czechoslovakia Svaty Mikalas) is thought to climb down to earth from heaven on a golden rope, accompanied by an angel and a devil who carries a whip.

A very old tradition in Czechoslovakia and Poland involves cutting a branch from a cherry tree and forcing it to bloom for Christmas by bringing it indoors and putting it in water. If the blooms are open in time for Christmas it is taken as a token of good luck, and it is also a harbinger of spring at a time of year when spring may seem discouragingly far off.

One of the most elaborate Christmas Eve traditions is the Polish celebration known as *Wigilia*. As in other countries, it falls within a period of meatless fasting and for many it concludes a twenty-four-hour period of strict fast. Thus everyone, especially the children, is most anxious for the feast to begin. Yet in commemoration of the star of Bethlehem, tradition says that the dinner may not begin until the first star of the night is seen. (The star is so important that though Christmas is officially known as *Bozz Narodzenie*, it is almost universally referred to as *Gwiazdka*, which means "little star.") Even after the first star is finally spot-

ted, no food may be consumed until *oplatek*, a special rice wafer blessed by the parish priest, has been broken in bits and served to everyone. It is also customary for the table be set with an even number of dishes for an odd number of guests, thus allowing an extra setting for the Holy Spirit.

CHRISTMAS CARP

Carp is a Christmas Eve delicacy among the Catholics of many Eastern European countries. In Poland carp is a symbol of strength and it is often eaten during Lent. But the most elaborate preparations, like the one below, are reserved for Christmas and New Year's. This recipe is a Bohemian specialty.

4-pound carp
1 tablespoon salt
2 cups water
1 cup dark beer or ale
1 carrot, scraped and sliced
1 stalk celery with leaves, sliced
1 leek, cleaned and sliced
1 small onion, roughly chopped
Small handful of parsley
¼ cup red wine vinegar
1 bay leaf
6 gingersnaps, crushed
½ cup blanched almonds, coarsely chopped
8 prunes, pitted and chopped
⅓ cup golden raisins
2 tablespoons brown sugar

Ask your fish merchant to clean the carp and remove the head but reserve it and take it home. Cut the carp into steaks 1 to 1½ inch thick. Sprinkle the fish with salt and let stand for 45 minutes.

In a saucepan, combine the carp head, water, beer or ale, carrot, celery, leek, onion, parsley, vinegar and bay leaf. Bring to a boil, turn the heat to low and simmer for 30 minutes. Remove from heat and strain the stock. Discard the carp head and vegetables.

Rinse and dry the salted carp steaks. Add to the strained stock and simmer gently for 25 to 30 minutes, until done. With a slotted spoon remove the fish steaks to a platter. Add the crushed gingersnaps, almond, prunes, raisins and sugar to the stock. Simmer, stirring frequently, for 10 minutes or until mixture has thickened slightly. Taste for seasoning and add vinegar, sugar or salt as needed. Pour the sauce over the fish and serve.

Yield: 6 servings.

NOODLES WITH POPPY SEEDS AND BUTTER

This is a traditional dish on Christmas Eve tables in many Eastern European countries. It is a very comforting dish and children love it.

8 ounces wide egg noodles
½ cup poppy seeds
4 tablespoons sugar
4 tablespoons unsalted butter
½ cup raisins

Bring a large quantity of water to the boil and cook the egg noodles until tender, about 10 minutes.

In a mortar and pestle pound the poppy seeds to a paste together with the sugar.

Drain the noodles and transfer to a large serving bowl. Toss them with the butter and ground poppy seeds with sugar. Finally toss in the raisins and mix well.

Yield: 4 to 6 servings.

MUSHROOM USZKI (MUSHROOM DUMPLINGS)

Uszki means "little ears," and that is what these mushroom-filled dumplings are thought to resemble.

Dough:

3½ cups all-purpose flour
2 eggs
1 cup water
1 teaspoon salt

Filling:

½ pound dried imported Polish mushrooms
1 onion
1 clove
Pinch of salt
1 stick unsalted butter
1 medium onion, finely chopped
¼ pound fresh mushrooms, finely chopped
¼ teaspoon thyme
½ cup fresh bread crumbs, preferably from a dark bread
1 tablespoon fresh dill, finely chopped
1 teaspoon salt
Freshly ground black pepper

In a saucepan combine the dried mushrooms with 1 quart of water. Add the onion, clove, and salt. Simmer for 1 hour.

In a bowl, mix together the flour, eggs, water, and salt to make a stiff but workable dough. Remove to a floured surface and knead until the dough feels smooth and elastic, about 10 minutes. Cover and let rest while you make the filling.

Drain the mushrooms and wash them carefully under cold running water. (You can strain the broth through several layers of cheesecloth or a paper coffee filter and freeze for use in soup or sauce.) Chop the mushrooms finely.

Melt the butter in a skillet. Add the chopped onion and sauté until wilted, about 10 minutes. Add all the mushrooms, thyme, bread crumbs, dill, salt, and lots of freshly ground black pepper. Sauté, stirring often, for 15 minutes. Let cool before using.

Cut the dough into four parts. Cover three parts while you roll out the fourth on a lightly floured surface. Roll out very thin, and cut out 2-inch squares. Place ½ teaspoon of filling a little to one side of each square. Pinch the edges together to form a triangle. Repeat until all dough and filling are used. As you make the uszki, place them on a well-floured cookie sheet. Make sure the dumplings do not touch each other. Cover with a flour-dredged towel. They can stand in a cool, dry place for several hours. (Uszki can be frozen at this point for future use.)

Bring 7 to 8 quarts of water to a boil. Drop in the uszki, about a dozen at a time. Simmer until they float to the top. Remove to a warm bowl and continue until all are done.

Yield: 80 to 90 uszki.

TWELVE-FRUIT COMPOTE

This compote is always the festive ending to the traditional *Wigilia*, the Polish Christmas Eve Feast. The twelve fruits in the compote symbolize the twelve apostles.

4 cups water
1 pound mixed dried fruit
1 cup pitted prunes
1 cup pitted cherries (canned or dried)
1 cup dried apples
1 cup cranberries
½ cup golden raisins
½ cup currants
½ cup sugar
1 lemon, very thinly sliced
4 cloves
1 cinnamon stick
1 cup mandarin orange sections (canned)
½ cup fresh or canned grapes
½ sliced banana
½ cup brandy, kirsch, or slivovitz

In a large saucepan combine the water, mixed dried fruit, prunes, cherries, apples, cranberries, raisins and currants. Add the sugar, lemon slices, cloves, and cinnamon. Bring to a boil and reduce heat to a simmer. Simmer for 20 minutes until all the fruit is soft.

Remove from heat and stir in mandarin orange sections, grapes, banana slices, and brandy, kirsch, or slivovitz.

Compote can be served warm or cold.

Yield: 12 to 14 servings.

PODKOVY (SWEET HORSESHOE-SHAPED ROLLS)

December 26 is St. Stephen's Day, and in Poland and other Slavic countries it is customary to bake these delicious sweet rolls shaped to resemble horseshoes—for St. Stephen's horse.

1 package active dry yeast
½ cup warm milk
3 eggs
1 cup sour cream
1 cup sugar
2 teaspoons lemon juice
Grated rind of 2 lemons
5 cups sifted all-purpose flour
¼ teaspoon salt
2 sticks unsalted butter, very cold, cut into small pieces
½ cup Crisco

Filling:

3 egg whites
1 cup sugar
¾ cup finely chopped nuts
½ cup chopped dried apricots
½ cup finely chopped pitted prunes
1 teaspoon vanilla extract

For top:

½ cup heavy cream
Confectioners' sugar

Sprinkle the yeast into the warm milk along with a pinch of sugar. Let stand for 5 to 10 minutes until frothy.

In a large bowl, beat the eggs until light and fluffy. Stir in sour cream, yeast mixture, sugar, and lemon juice and rind.

Combine flour and salt. With two knives or cold fingers work the butter and Crisco into the flour until the mixture resembles a coarse meal. (You can also do this in a food processor. Work with 2½ cups flour at a time with half the butter and Crisco.) Add the flour/butter mixture to the liquid mixture and enough more flour if necessary to make a soft but workable dough. Scoop the dough into a ball, wrap in plastic, and chill in refrigerator for 1 hour.

Combine all the ingredients for the filling and mix well.

Preheat oven to 375°F. Lightly grease a baking sheet with butter or vegetable shortening.

On a lightly floured surface roll the dough until about ⅛ inch thick. Cut dough into 4-inch squares or cut out 4-inch circles. Spread 1 heaping teaspoon of filling on each square or circle. Roll up starting from a corner and shape into a crescent (or horseshoe). Place on prepared baking sheet. Brush tops with heavy cream and bake for 20 minutes, until golden brown. The dough will rise as the rolls bake. Remove from oven and cool on wire racks. Dust with confectioners' sugar before serving.

Yield: 2 to 3 dozen horseshoes.

BARSZ WITH MUSHROOM UZSKI

Barsz is borscht, meatless in this case for Christmas Eve but much enlivened by the little mushroom *uzski* (dumplings) that float on top.

2 quarts water
2 medium onions, chopped
2 leeks, cleaned and chopped
2 carrots, chopped
1 turnip, peeled and chopped
½ head of cabbage, chopped
8 medium beets, scrubbed and left whole
2 cloves garlic, peeled and smashed
Fistful of parsley with root if possible
1 teaspoon salt
1 tablespoon red wine vinegar
1 bay leaf
6 peppercorns
Mushroom Uszki (following recipe)
Juice of ½ lemon
¼ cup fresh dill, chopped

In a large pot, combine the water with the onions, leeks, carrots, turnip, cabbage, beets, garlic, parsley, salt, red wine vinegar, bay leaf, and peppercorns. Bring to a boil, reduce heat and simmer for 1 hour. Remove from heat and strain the broth.

Discard all the vegetables except the beets. When beets are cool enough to handle, peel them and cut into julienne. Return to broth. Prepare the uzski.

Heat the borscht and taste for seasoning. Add more salt if necessary and add the lemon juice. Float 3 or 4 uszki in each plate of barsz.

Yield: 6 to 8 servings.

How to Say Merry Christmas in Thirty-seven Languages

Afrikaner: Een Plesierige Kerfees
Argentinian: Felices Pasquas y felices Ano Nuevo
Armenian: Schernorhavor Dzenount
Bohemian: Vesele Vanoce
Bulgarian: Chestita Koleda
Chinese: Kung Hsi Hsin Niene bing Chu Shen Tan
Croatian: Sretan Bozic
Danish: Glaedelig Jul
Esperanto: Gajan Kristnaskon
Estonian: Roomsaid Joulu Puhi
Finnish: Houska Joulua
Flemish: Vrolike Kerstmis
French: Joyeux Noël
German: Froehliche Weihnachten
Greek: Kala Christougena
Dutch: Vrolyk Kerfeest en Gelukkig Nieuw Jaar
Hungarian: Kellemes Karacsonyi unnepeket
Iraqian: Idah Saidan Wa Sanah Jadidah
Irish: Nodlaig mhaith chugnat
Italian: Buon Natale
Japanese: Meri Kurisumasu
Jugoslavian: Cestitamo Bozic
Lettish: Priecigus Ziemassvetkus
Lithuanian: Linksmu Kaledu
Norwegian: God Jul og Godt Nytt Aar
Polish: Boze Narodzenie
Portuguese: Boas Festas y Feliz Ano Novo
Rumanian: Sarbatori vesele
Russian: S Rozhdestvom Kristovym
Serbian: Hristos se rodi
Slovakian: Vesele vianoce
Spanish: Feliz Navidad
Swedish: God Jul
Turkish: Noeliniz Ve Yeni Yiliniz Kutlu Olsun
Ukrainian: Chrystos Rozdzajetsia Slawyte Jeho
Welsh: Nadolig Llawen

CHRISTMAS
IN
CANADA

Canada, like the United States, is a large melting pot whose population consists largely of immigrants from all over the world. As a result, Christmas celebrations are as varied as the people themselves and reflect the rich and varied backgrounds of Canadians.

In Quebec, where French traditions are foremost, preparations for Christmas begin weeks before, as menus are planned, visits are arranged, and houses are decorated. The Christmas tree is trimmed and a crèche is set up, usually under the tree. A star sits atop the tree as a symbol of the star of Bethlehem, which guided the three Magi on their quest. Christmas Eve dinner is a meatless meal and usually involves the preparation of seafood. Then everyone attends the *messe de minuit* (midnight Mass), where another crèche is usually displayed before the church altar. Some families open their gifts right after the midnight Mass, others wait for New Year's Day to discover what presents Père Noël has brought from the Christ Child.

Le Réveillon is the main feast of Christmas. It takes place in the wee hours of the morning following the midnight Mass, and since it breaks a meatless fast of some weeks' duration, it is customarily elaborate, featuring *tourtiere* (meat pie), stuffed turkey, or goose, vegetables and salad, with fruitcake or a *bûche de Noël* for dessert.

For the Métis, descendants of French and Indian mixed marriages, Christmas Eve is just the beginning of a two week celebration that involves religious ceremonies and is almost always the occasion for huge family reunions. The men fire their guns in the meadows to signal the beginning of the festivities. Gifts are exchanged around the fire, and everyone wears his finest attire, including hand-made moccasins and arrow-figured belts. The traditional meal, consisting of wild game, the choicest cuts of buffalo, deer, and moose along with berries, potatoes, and wild rice—recalls the Christmases celebrated by the *coureurs des bois*, trappers of earlier times. After the meal, there is fiddling, dancing, singing, and winter games, especially sleigh rides and horseback riding.

German immigrants to Canada take pride in the fact that they introduced the illuminated Christmas tree to Canada, where

> Dame, get up and bake your pies
> bake your pies, bake your pies
> Dame get up and bake your pies,
> On Christmas Day in the morning.
>
> Traditional English song

it became a popular tradition. The German-born General Friedrich-Adolph von Riedesel was in command of the Brunswick regiment that fought on the side of the British during the American War of Independence. In 1781 he commanded all British troops from Sorel to Montreal. He and his wife and children moved into le Château des Gouverneurs, which still stands today, in Sorel, just a few days before Christmas 1781. There Mrs. von Riedesel decorated a pine tree in their reception hall with apples, gold-covered nuts, candy rings, ginger squares, and candles.

On Christmas Eve, some British officers and neighbors, along with their families, were invited to the tree-lighting ceremony. The tree-lighting custom spread rapidly through Quebec and then to the rest of Canada, probably owing to the fact that more than one thousand German soldiers married Quebec women and settled in Canada. Around 1850, Montreal newspapers reported that the Christmas tree was in common use all over Canada, which was considerably earlier than any other country outside Germany.

British settlers brought their own customs with them from England; they celebrate Christmas with traditional English dishes featuring a roast bird or beef, plum pudding, and mince pie. Where holly and mistletoe would have been the decorations in the old world, wintergreen and cranberry sprigs are substituted.

In Scottish communities, where people are part of a Presbyterian tradition, the gift giving and social activities take place on New Year's Day, following hogmanay (New Year's Eve).

TOURTIERE (MEAT PIE)

This tasty meat pie is traditional fare at Christmas celebrations all over French Canada and among the Acadians in Nova Scotia.

Pastry:

2½ cups all-purpose flour
¼ teaspoon salt
4 tablespoons unsalted butter
4 tablespoons lard or solid vegetable shortening
1 egg
6 to 8 tablespoons ice water
Additional butter for pie pan

Filling:

2 medium onions, finely chopped
1 clove garlic, finely minced
3 tablespoons butter
1 pound ground pork
1 pound ground veal
1 teaspoon allspice
½ teaspoon cinnamon
½ teaspoon savory
1 teaspoon salt
½ teaspoon freshly ground black pepper (or to taste)
1 bay leaf
1 cup beef broth or water
2 unbaked 9-inch pie shells with pastry for tops
2 to 3 tablespoons heavy cream

Make the pie pastry. Place flour and salt in the bowl of a food processor. Add the butter, cut into small pieces, and the lard or vegetable shortening. Pulse on and off until mixture resembles a coarse meal. With the processor on add the water, 1 tablespoon at a time, until the dough forms into a ball. Gather the ball, wrap it in plastic and refrigerate for 30 minutes. (You can make the pastry the day before and refrigerate overnight.)

Prepare the filling. Melt the butter in a large skillet and sauté the onion and garlic until soft and wilted, about 15 minutes, but do not let them brown. Add the pork and veal and cook, stirring and breaking up the meat, until it has lost some of its raw color. Stir in the allspice, cinnamon, savory, salt, pepper, bay leaf, and broth or water. Cook over medium heat, stirring frequently, for 30 minutes until mixture is fairly dry. Taste for seasoning, remove the bay leaf and allow mixture to cool to room temperature.

Preheat oven to 350°F.

Rub the insides of an 11-inch pie pan with butter. Divide the dough into two parts, one slightly larger than the other. Roll out the larger piece of dough into a circle big enough to line the bottom and sides of the pie pan. Place the dough into the pan, cut off the excess edges, and pierce the bottom all over with the tines of a fork.

Spread the meat mixture in the pie shell. Roll out remaining dough into a circle and cover with a top crust. Seal the edges and prick the top with the tines of a fork to allow steam to escape. Brush the top crusts with heavy cream. You can decorate the top crust with any remaining scraps of pastry. Bake at 350°F. for 45 to 50 minutes, until the top is golden and crusty.

Let cool before slicing. Many Canadians consider that the flavor of the pie improves if it is allowed to cool, and is refrigerated overnight and reheated. To reheat, place in a 300°F. oven for 35 to 40 minutes.

Yield: 8 to 10 servings.

CANADIAN MAPLE PIE

A great Christmas dessert, when everyone knows that calories don't count.

4 tablespoons unsalted butter, at room temperature
½ cup sugar
3 large eggs
1 cup pure maple syrup
1 cup pecans, coarsely chopped
1 9-inch unbaked pie shell
1 cup heavy cream
½ teaspoon sugar

Preheat oven to 400°F.

Cream butter and sugar together until very light and fluffy. Beat in eggs, one at a time, until mixture is frothy and light lemon colored. Beat in the maple syrup. Fold in the chopped pecans. Turn the mixture into the unbaked pie shell. Bake at 400°F. for 40 to 45 minutes, until the filling is set and crust is golden. Remove from oven and cool on wire rack.

Whip the cream together with the sugar until peaks form. Serve pie at room temperature or chilled, with a dollop of whipped cream.

Yield: 8 servings.

HOGMANAY SHORTBREAD

Hogmanay is the Scottish New Year's Eve, and the serving of shortbread to those who go visiting from house to house has long been a custom among Canadians of Scottish descent. This recipe is adapted from a charming book called *Out of Old Nova Scotia Kitchens*, by Marie Nightingale.

3 cups all-purpose flour
½ cup sugar
2 sticks unsalted butter, very cold
1 to 2 tablespoons cold milk

Preheat oven to 275°F.

Sift the butter and sugar together. Cut the butter into small pieces and rub the butter into the flour-sugar mixture until the mixture resembles a coarse meal. Alternately, place the flour-sugar mixture into the bowl of a food processor and add the butter, cut into small pieces. Process until mixture resembles a coarse meal. Knead with your hands for about 5 minutes until mixture forms a ball. Divide in two and shape each piece into a flat round cake 1 inch thick. Place in two 9-inch metal pie plates and press out to form cakes about ½-inch thick. Pinch the edges and prick all over with the tines of a fork. Bake at 275°F. for 1 hour, or until cake is lightly browned. Remove from oven and leave in pie plates until shortbead is completely cooled. Serve in pieces broken off from cooled cake, or cut into wedges while still hot. Store in a tightly covered tin or plastic box, in a cool, dry place.

Yield: 2 shortbreads.

St. Nicholas to Santa Claus

As we have seen, Christmas is a holiday as varied in its observance across the world as it is universal among Christians. Yet common to all Christmas observances is a spirit of rejoicing and magnanimity. Gift giving, especially for children, is the custom almost everywhere, and everywhere too a figure is associated with the season who is the embodiment of the gift-giving spirit. In this country he is best known as Santa Claus, but he is a ubiquitous fellow with many names, and his history is a history of the crosscurrents of cultures and customs.

The English Santa Claus, Old Father Christmas, dates back at least to the fifteenth century. A woodcut dating from 1653 portrays him in a costume not very different from his modern attire. But the fat, jolly, white-bearded modern Santa Claus, the reindeer-driving, chimney-climbing stocking stuffer, was invented in the United States, a pastiche of myths and beliefs including Norse and Russian legends of wizards living at the North Pole, the historical Nicholas, bishop of Myra, and Kriss Kringle, a German-American folk figure who punishes bad children and rewards the good. In 1823 the enormous popularity of Clement Moore's *A Visit from St. Nicholas* forged these and other converging elements into the modern concept of Santa Claus, at least in the English-speaking world.

Dutch children get their holiday gifts from Sinte Klaas or St. Nicholas on his feast day, December 6. He's a long-bearded fellow in white robe and crimson cassock, tall red mitre, and gold crozier, all of which is fitting, since in Dutch tradition he is associated with the fourth-century Bishop of Myra, who was born in Spain. Each year he and his Moorish servant, Zwarte Piet, or

St. Nicholas is the patron saint of Russia and Greece as well as of the following groups: children, poor children, sick children, maidens, judges, murderers, pawnbrokers, thieves, merchants, paupers, sailors, scholars, and people in trouble anywhere.

Black Peter, are thought to travel from Spain to Amsterdam and to visit each house, where Zwarte Piet draws from his enormous black bag either gifts for the good children or switches to punish the naughty. Children are told that if they are very bad indeed, Zwarte Piet will spirit them away in his bag and keep them in Spain for a year before returning them, presumably well chastened, to their parents the following Christmas. The Netherlands were under Spanish control in the sixteenth century, which no doubt contributed to the tradition.

In many parts of Holland, December 5 is known as Strewing Eve because of the following tradition: Early in the evening, before guests arrive, a knock is heard at the door, which then opens just wide enough to admit a black-gloved hand thought to belong Black Peter. The hand tosses hard round spice cookies called *pepernoten*, on the floor.

Later that night St. Nicholas and Black Peter visit the rooftops of every house, though it is Black Peter alone who slips down the chimney, so that St. Nicholas will not soil his fine white robes with soot. Like the stockings that are hung by the mantel with care in other traditions, wooden shoes are put out near the chimney by Dutch children. In the morning the shoes are discovered filled up with traditional gifts like pink and white candy hearts; spiced honey gingerbreads, cut into human and animal shapes; and often immense gingerbread figures of St. Nicholas on his horse, or Black Peter with his bag.

In France as well, St. Nicholas has a companion, Père Fouettard. (They too arrive on St. Nicholas's feast day, December 6.) Père Fouettard, like Zwarte Piet in the Netherlands, carries a bundle of switches, and is thought to know just exactly and in detail who has been naughty or nice. A switch is left for the naughty ones, and if they have been very bad, there is always the awful chance that St. Nicholas will skip over their house when he passes out gifts.

In Luxembourg St. Nicholas is accompanied by Hoesecker, who carries switches and never hesitates to whip the lazy or disobedient child. In Czechoslovakia, it is St. Mikulase (the same old Nicholas, really) who brings presents on December 6. He comes down from heaven on a golden cord carrying on his back a basket of apples, nuts, and candies.

Cookies for St. Nicholas

Small cakes and cookies, including those used in the eucharist, have a long history of association with religious rites and rituals. In many of the earliest religions, animal sacrifice was considered essential to influence or mollify the gods. But at some point in the development of most cultures, the sacrifices became symbolic rather than literal. In China a story is told that in olden days when one particularly angry god demanded a human sacrifice, there was a great deal of shuffling of feet but very little in the way of volunteering. Eventually someone hit upon the brilliant idea of offering a gingerbread man instead, and apparently the god was not displeased.

The idea had a lot of practical appeal. Among the ancient Germans it was the custom to sacrifice live horses to the king of their gods, Wotan. All very well for rich chieftains, perhaps, but for poorer folk, who had no horses, it became customary to give horse-shaped cookies instead. Indeed, the cookie, called *Springerle* (which means "little jumper") is still made at Christmastime today and offered no longer to Wotan but to Kriss Kringle, The Christ Child. Springerle and literally hundreds of other cookies, many of them cut out or imprinted with wonderfully carved molds, have long since become associated with the Yule festvities.

Today in many parts of the world the arrival of St. Nicholas on December 6 is inseparably associated with the beginning of the Christmas season and, inevitably, with the baking of cookies. Many are traditionally left as sweet inducements for St. Nicholas to visit, while others are supposedly delivered by him and his various helpers as rewards for good behavior. In any case, December 7 is none too soon to start baking some of these traditional Christmas cookies.

Christmas is coming, the geese are getting fat,
Please to put a penny in the old man's hat;
If you haven't got a penny, a ha'penny will do,
If you haven't got a ha'penny, God bless you!

—Beggar's rhyme

Speculaas (Molded Spice Cookies)

Dutch speculaas are Christmas spice cookies particularly associated with St. Nicholas and often baked in portrait molds of his image. These cookies take their name—*speculaas* is a Dutch variation of *speculum*, the Latin word for "mirror"—from the traditional method of shaping them. Carved wooden molds are pressed into the rolled cookie dough, and then the "mirrored" shapes are cut out and baked. In the absence of a traditional speculaas mold, a springerle rolling pin or board can be substituted (see following recipe). Or simply cut into squares and bake.

2 sticks unsalted butter, at room temperature
1½ cups brown sugar
2 large eggs
1 tablespoon grated lemon rind
1 tablespoon cinnamon
1 teaspoon cloves
1 teaspoon nutmeg
½ teaspoon cardamom
½ teaspoon black pepper
4 cups all-purpose flour, sifted
4 teaspoons baking powder
½ teaspoon salt
¼ cup milk, approximately
½ cup blanched slivered almonds

Preheat oven to 350°F. Grease several sheets with butter or solid vegetable shortening.

Cream butter and sugar together until very light and fluffy. Beat in eggs, one at a time, until mixture is frothy and pale lemon-colored. Beat in the lemon rind, cinnamon, cloves, nutmeg, cardamom, and pepper.

Sift the flour together with baking powder and salt and stir into the butter and egg mixture. Add enough milk to make a smooth, soft dough.

Roll the dough out on a lightly floured surface to a thickness of about ½ inch. Either press patterns into the dough with a lightly floured speculaas board, or simply cut the dough into 3-inch squares.

Place the cookies on prepared baking sheets and decorate each cookie with slivered almonds, pressing them lightly into the dough. Bake at 350°F. for 15 to 20 minutes, until cookies are golden brown. Remove cookies from oven and cool on wire racks. Store cookies in an airtight container.

Yield: about 3½ dozen cookies.

CHRISTMAS SUGAR COOKIES

1 pound (4 sticks) unsalted butter, softened to room temperature
2 cups sugar
2 large eggs
1 tablespoon vanilla extract
1 cup finely ground almonds
5 cups all-purpose flour
1 teaspoon baking soda
Pinch of salt
½ cup sugar
1 teaspoon freshly grated nutmeg

Cream butter and sugar together until very light and fluffy. Beat in eggs one at a time until mixture is very frothy and lemon-colored. Beat in vanilla.

Stir in ground almonds. Sift together flour, baking soda, and salt. Stir into the creamed mixture to make a smooth dough that leaves the sides of the bowl. Scoop up into a ball, wrap in plastic, and chill for 1 hour before using. (Can be refrigerated overnight.)

Preheat oven to 375°F. Grease several cookie sheets with butter or vegetable shortening. Mix together the ½ cup sugar with freshly grated nutmeg.

Divide the dough in half or even quarters to make rolling out easier. Chill the dough that is waiting to be rolled out. Roll out the dough as thin as possible on a lightly floured surface. Cut out into your favorite cookie shaps. Arrange cookies on prepared cookie sheets. Dust the tops lightly with nutmeg-flavored sugar. Bake for 8 to 10 minutes. Cool on wire racks. Store in an airtight container in a cool place. These keep well for several weeks.

Yield: 5 to 6 dozen cookies.

VARIATIONS: You can omit the ground almonds or substitute ground walnuts or any other nuts of your choice. You can substitute 1 teaspoon cinnamon for the grated nutmeg in the sugar topping.

In some areas of Europe the St. Nicholas Day procession features a cart with the figures of three boys riding in a salt barrel. This refers to the legend that dates back to the fourth century, when the historical Nicholas was bishop of Myra, in Asia Minor. It seems that the three sons of an Oriental nobleman—schoolboys on holiday, as the story has it—were traveling through the town. Arriving late, and intending to call on the bishop as their father had requested, the boys decided to spend the night at a local inn.

The landlord, it turned out, was in need of meat for his customers and being somewhat unscrupulous about its source, he killed the boys in their sleep and pickled them in brine.

That night the heinous crime was revealed to St. Nicholas in a dream. Waking from the dream he hurried to the inn, where he denounced the landlord and brought the boys back to life. Because of this story Nicholas has been known as the patron saint of all children, but particularly of schoolboys.

Another story told about the bishop of Myra concerns a man who, having lost all his money, was unable to provide a proper dowry for his three daughters, and thought they must surely become prostitutes, for without a dowry they could not hope to marry, and without money he could not hope to support them. Hearing of the man's situation, Nicholas is said to have thrown into the man's house three separate bags of gold to make dowries for the daughters.

Possibly these stories help to explain why St. Nicholas is, among other things, the patron saint of children and unmarried women.

SPRINGERLE

This German Christmas cookie is rolled out with a traditional springerle rolling pin or on a springerle board. These are engraved with a variety of Christmas symbols and pictures. If you do not have a springerle rolling pin or board, simply roll out with a regular rolling pin and cut out the dough with cookie cutters or into 2-inch squares. These cookies should be baked several weeks before Christmas because they improve with keeping. The dough itself should be prepared the day before baking the cookies.

4 cups flour
1 teaspoon baking powder
4 large eggs
2 cups sugar
2 teaspoons grated lemon rind
2 teaspoons whole anise extract

In a large bowl sift together the 3½ cups of flour and the baking powder. In another bowl, beat the eggs until they are lemon-colored and very fluffy. Gradually beat in the sugar until the mixture is smooth and creamy. Beat in the lemon rind and anise extract.

Beat the 3½ cups of flour into the egg mixture a little at a time to make a stiff dough. Roll the dough into a ball, wrap in plastic, and chill until very firm, about two hours.

Grease several cookie sheets with butter and line with baking parchment.

Spread the remaining ½ cup flour on a flat surface or on a pastry cloth. Roll out the cookie dough on the floured surface until it is about ½ inch thick. Sprinkle the springerle board or rolling pin with flour and press into the rolled out dough. Cut rolled out dough into patterns made by springerle board or rolling pin, or cut out dough with cookie cutters, or cut into 2-inch squares. Arrange cookies on the prepared cookie sheets. Let unbaked cookies stand at room temperature for 12 hours before baking.

Preheat oven to 325°F.

Bake for 30 minutes. Cookies should be light on top and slightly golden on the bottom. Remove cookies to wire rack and cool completely before storing in an airtight container.

Yield: about 50 cookies.

Baseler Leckerli (Basel Treats)

In Switzerland these honey spice cookies are shaped with special leckerli molds. You can use a springerle mold or rolling pin, or simply cut the cookies into bars. In any case, these cookies should "ripen" for a full month before being eaten.

Prepare the cookie dough 2 to 3 days before baking cookies.

1½ cups honey
⅓ cup kirsch
½ cup brown sugar
¼ cup candied lemon peel, roughly chopped
¼ cup candied orange peel, roughly chopped
Grated rind of 1 lemon
1 tablespoon cinnamon
1 teaspoon allspice
1 teaspoon grated nutmeg
1 cup coarsely ground almonds
3½ cups flour, approximately
1 teaspoon baking soda
Pinch of salt
White Sugar Icing, (following recipe)

In a large saucepan, heat the honey until almost boiling. Turn off heat. Stir in kirsch and sugar. Cook, stirring, over very low heat until the sugar is completely dissolved. Remove from heat and stir in the candied lemon peel, candied orange peel, grated lemon rind, cinnamon, allspice, and nutmeg. Remove to a large mixing bowl. Stir in the ground almonds.

Sift the flour with the baking soda and salt. Stir flour mixture into the honey mixture to make a very stiff dough. If necessary, stir in more flour until the dough is thick enough to leave the sides of the bowl. Cover the bowl with plastic wrap and let it stand in a cool place for 2 to 3 days.

Preheat oven to 350°F. Grease several cookie sheets with butter or vegetable shortening. Dust with flour and tap off the excess.

Remove cookie dough to a lightly floured surface and roll out to a thickness of ¼ inch. Press shapes into cookie dough with leckerli or springerle molds or cut into 2- by 3-inch bars. Arrange cookies on prepared cookie sheets and bake in a 350°F. for 20 to 25 minutes, until golden brown.

Remove from oven and brush the cookies with White Sugar Icing while they are still warm. When completely cold, store in an airtight container for about 4 weeks before eating.

Yield: about 3 dozen cookies.

White Sugar Icing

3 to 4 cups confectioners' sugar
4 tablespoons boiling water, approximately
½ teaspoon vanilla extract
Rum or brandy

Place the sugar in a bowl and gradually stir in enough boiling water to make a thick paste. Stir in vanilla and enough rum or brandy to thin icing to desired consistency.

Yield: about 2 cups.

LEBKUCHEN (GERMAN HONEY CAKES)

"Leb-" is derived from the Latin *libum*, which was a consecrated cake used in Roman religious ceremonies. Lebkuchen means "sacred cakes." In Germany and Switzerland these Christmas cakes are often baked in elaborate, beautifully carved molds.

1 pound honey
1 cup sugar
4 large eggs
½ cup strong black coffee
1 cup blanched slivered almonds
½ cup citron, roughly chopped
¼ cup candied orange peel
Grated rind from 2 lemons
2 teaspoons cinnamon
1 teaspoon anise seeds, lightly crushed
½ teaspoon clove
½ teaspoon grated nutmeg
1½ teaspoons baking powder
4 cups flour, approximately

In a heavy saucepan, heat the honey until very hot and thinned out. Stir in sugar and keep stirring over low heat until all the sugar is completely dissolved. Remove from heat and let cool. Pour into a large mixing bowl and beat in the eggs, one at a time, until each is completely absorbed. Beat in coffee. Stir in almonds, citron, candied orange peel, grated lemon rind, cinnamon, anise, cloves, and nutmeg. Sift flour together with baking powder and stir into the liquid mixture to make a smooth dough. Cover and let stand in a cool place to ripen overnight or for several days.

Preheat oven to 375°F. Grease several baking sheets with butter or vegetable shortening.

Remove dough to a lightly floured surface and knead briefly, adding a bit more flour if necessary to make a rollable dough. Roll out to a thickness of ¼ inch. Cut into 2-by-3-inch rectangles or into circles or hearts. Arrange on prepared baking sheets and bake for 15 to 20 minutes, until golden brown. Cool on wire racks. Decorate with White Sugar Icing, page 115, if you wish. These keep for a long time, stored in an airtight container in a cool place.

Yield: about 3 dozen cookies.

BUTTER COOKIES

This is the perfect dough for your favorite cookie cutter shapes.

1 stick plus 4 tablespoons unsalted butter, at room temperature
1 cup sugar
2 eggs
1 teaspoon vanilla extract
2 cups all-purpose flour
1 teaspoon baking powder
1 egg white beaten with 1 tablespoon water
Colored sugar

Cream the butter and sugar together until very light and fluffy. Beat in eggs one at a time until mixture is very frothy and lemon-colored. Beat in vanilla extract. Sift together the flour and baking powder and stir into the creamed mixture. Knead briefly to make a smooth dough. Scoop into a ball, wrap in plastic, and chill for 1 hour or overnight.

Preheat oven to 375°F. Grease a baking sheet with butter or vegetable shortening.

Remove cookie dough to a lightly floured surface and roll out very thin, between ¼ and ⅛ inch. Cut out your favorite cookie shapes. Arrange cookies on prepared baking sheet, brush with egg white beaten with water, and sprinkle with colored sugar.

Bake 10 to 12 minutes, until just turning golden. Cool on wire racks.

Yield: about 2½ dozen cookies.

Lemon Butter Cookies

1 stick unsalted butter, softened to room temperature
1 cup sugar
1 egg
1 tablespoon fresh lemon juice
1 teaspoon vanilla extract
Grated rind of 1 lemon
1¼ cups all-purpose flour

Cream butter and sugar together until very light and fluffy. Beat in the egg, lemon juice, and vanilla extract. Stir in grated lemon rind and flour. Knead briefly to make a smooth dough. Scoop into a ball, cover with plastic, and refrigerate for several hours or overnight.

Preheat oven to 375°F.

Remove cookie dough to a lightly floured surface and roll out very thin, about ¼ inch. Cut out 2-inch circles or any other favorite shape. Arrange cookie on ungreased cookie sheet.

Bake at 375°F. for 8 to 10 minutes, until edges just start to brown. Cool on wire racks.

Yield: about 3 dozen cookies.

Moravian Christmas Cookies

1 stick unsalted butter
1 cup brown sugar
¼ cup heavy cream
1 cup molasses
1½ teaspoons cinnamon
1 teaspoon ginger
¼ teaspoon grated nutmeg
3½ to 4 cups flour

Preheat oven to 325°F. Grease several baking sheets with butter or vegetable shortening. Dust with flour and knock off excess.

Cream butter and sugar together until very light and fluffy. Beat in the cream, molasses, cinnamon, ginger, and nutmeg. Gradually stir in the flour to make a smooth, rather stiff dough. Roll out dough on lightly floured surface until very thin, about ⅛ inch. Cut out shapes with your favorite cookie cutters and arrange on prepared baking sheets. Bake 10 to 12 minutes, until cookies just start to turn color. Cool on wire racks. Store in airtight container. These cookies keep well for several weeks.

Yield: 3½ to 4 dozen cookies.

A Visit from St. Nicholas

by Clement Moore

'Twas the night before Christmas, when all through the house
Not a creature was stirring, not even a mouse;
The stockings were hung by the chimney with care,
In hopes that St. Nicholas soon would be there;
The children were nestled all snug in their beds,
While visions of sugar-plums danced in their heads;
And mama in her kerchief, and I in my cap,
Had just settled down for a long winter's nap,
when out on the lawn there arose such a clatter,
I sprang from my bed to see what was the matter.
Away to the window I flew with a flash,
Tore open the shutters and threw up the sash.
The moon on the crest of the new-fallen snow,
Gave the luster of mid-day to objects below,
When, what to my wondering eyes should appear,
But a miniature sleigh, and eight tiny reindeer.
With a little old driver, so lively and quick
I knew in a moment it must be St. Nick.
More rapid than eagles his coursers they came,
And he whistled and shouted and called them by name:
"Now, Dasher! now, Dancer! now, Prancer and Vixen!
On, Comet! on, Cupid! on Donner and Blitzen!
To the top of the porch, to the top of the wall!
Now, dash away, dash away, dash away all!"
As dry leaves that before the wild hurricane fly,
When they meet with an obstacle, mount to the sky,
So, up to the house-top the coursers they flew,
With a sleigh full of toys,—and St. Nicholas too.
And then in a twinkling I heard on the roof
The prancing and pawing of each little hoof.
As I drew in my head and was turning around,
Down the chimney St. Nicholas came with a bound.
He was dressed all in fur from his head to his foot,
And his clothes were all tarnished with ashes and soot;
A bundle of toys he had flung on his back,
And he looked like a peddler just opening his pack.
His eyes how they twinkled! his dimples how merry!
His cheeks were like roses, his nose like a cherry;
His droll little mouth was drawn up like a bow,
And the beard on his chin was as white as the snow.
The stump of a pipe he held tight in his teeth,
And the smoke it encircled his head like a wreath.
He had a broad face, and a little round belly

That shook, when he laughed, like a bowl full of jelly.
He was chubby and plump—a right jolly old elf—
And I laughed when I saw him, in spite of myself.
A wink of his eye and a twist of his head
Soon gave me to know I had nothing to dread.
He spoke not a word, but went straight to his work,
And filled all the stockings; then turned with a jerk,
And laying his finger aside of his nose,
And giving a nod, up the chimney he rose.
He sprang to his sleigh, to his team gave a whistle,
And away they all flew like the down of a thistle;
But I heard him exclaim, ere he drove out of sight:
"Happy Christmas to all, and to all a good-night."

LUCIAPEPPERKAKOR (LUCIA GINGER SNAPS)

In Sweden these ginger snaps are baked for St. Lucy's Day, December 13. The dough is very easy to work with and it is fun to use your fanciest and most whimsical cookie cutters. A good cookie to bake with children throughout the Christmas holiday.

½ cup dark corn syrup
½ cup molasses
2 cups brown sugar
1 tablespoon ginger
Grated rind of 1 lemon
2 tablespoons baking soda
1½ cups heavy cream
7 to 8 cups all-purpose flour
Fancy Sugar Icing (recipe follows)

In a small, heavy saucepan, heat the corn syrup and molasses. Stir in sugar, ginger, grated lemon rind, and baking soda. Stir until all the sugar has dissolved. Remove from heat.

In a large bowl whip the heavy cream until it is almost stiff. Gradually, stir the syrup mixture into the whipped cream. Beat at low speed with an electric mixer for 5 minutes (twice as long if beating by hand). Stir in 5 cups of flour and mix well. Stir in the remaining flour a little at a time to make a soft dough. It should be smooth enough to handle and very pliable. Knead the dough briefly (2 to 3 minutes), scoop up into a ball, wrap in plastic, and refrigerate for several hours or overnight.

Preheat oven to 275°F. Grease several cookie sheets with butter or vegetable shortening.

Roll out the dough on a lightly floured surface to a thickness of ¼ inch. Cut with cookie cutters into fancy shapes. Place the cookies on prepared cookie sheets and bake at 275°F. for about 12 minutes, until cookies are golden brown. Cool on wire racks and decorate with Fancy Sugar Icing.

Yield: about 5 dozen cookies.

FANCY SUGAR ICING

2 egg whites, at room temperature
Pinch of salt
2 cups confectioners' sugar, approximately
1 teaspoon lemon juice
Food coloring (optional)

Beat the egg whites together with the salt until very frothy. Beat in the confectioners' sugar and lemon juice until stiff peaks are formed. If necessary add a little more sugar to make a stiff paste. Divide into portions for different colors and add a few drops of food coloring to each portion. Fill a pastry tube half full with icing and pipe the icing through a narrow tube onto cooled cookies. Or spread icing with a knife or spatula.

Yield: about 1½ cups.

Spritz Cookies

The name for these cookies comes from the German word *spritzen*, meaning "to squirt," because the soft dough is pushed, or squirted, through a cookie press to make fancy designs. If you don't have a cookie press or gun, use a pastry bag with a large star tip.

2 sticks unsalted butter, at room temperature
3/4 cup sugar
1 large egg
1 teaspoon vanilla or almond extract
2 1/2 cups all-purpose flour
1/2 teaspoon baking powder

Preheat oven to 375°F.

Cream together the butter and sugar until very light and fluffy. Beat in the egg and vanilla or almond extract. Sift together the flour and baking powder and stir into creamed mixture. Put the dough through a cookie press or a pastry bag fitted with a large star and press out onto an ungreased cookie sheet, spacing cookies about 1 inch apart.

Bake for 8 to 10 minutes, until cookies are golden brown. Remove from oven and cool on wire racks.

Yield: about 5 dozen cookies.

Christmas Ice Box Cookies

Make the dough for these delicious cookies at your leisure and keep it on hand in the refrigerator or freezer to slice and bake whenever you want. The dough will keep perfectly well in the refrigerator for up to a week and for months in the freezer.

2 sticks unsalted butter, at room temperature
1 cup sugar
2 large eggs
2 teaspoons vanilla extract
3 cups flour
1 teaspoon baking soda
1/2 teaspoon salt

For decorating the cookies choose one of the following:

Your favorite jam
Pecan halves
Colored sprinkles

Cream together the butter and sugar until very light and fluffy. Beat in eggs one at a time, then beat in vanilla extract. Sift together the flour, baking soda, and salt. Stir into the creamed mixture to make a smooth dough.

Divide the dough into four equal parts and roll into logs approximately 1 inch in diameter. Wrap in plastic and refrigerate for several hours, overnight, or longer. The cookie logs may be frozen until ready to use.

Preheat oven to 375°F. Grease a cookie sheet with butter or vegetable shortening.

Slice cookie logs into rounds approximately 1/4 inch thick and place on prepared cookie sheet, leaving a space of 1 inch between each cookie. To decorate, sprinkle with colored sprinkles or make an indentation in each cookie with your finger and place in it a bit of jam or a pecan half.

Bake at 375°F. for 10 to 12 minutes, until cookies are golden in color. Cool on wire racks.

Yield: about 5 dozen cookies.

Crescents

2 sticks unsalted butter, softened to room temperature
1 cup confectioners' sugar
1 teaspoon vanilla extract
1 teaspoon almond extract
1 cup blanched almonds, coarsely chopped
2½ cups all-purpose flour

Additional confectioners' sugar

Preheat oven to 350°F.

Cream butter and sugar together until very light and fluffy. Beat in vanilla and almond extract. Stir in almonds and flour to make a smooth dough. Knead very lightly to blend well.

Divide dough in half and shape dough into two long rolls about 1 inch diameter. Cut off pieces about 1 inch long and shape each into a 2-inch sausage, rolling the dough between the palms of your hands. Form into crescents and place on an ungreased cookie sheet.

Bake at 350° F. for 15 to 20 minutes, until cookies turn golden in color. Let stand until cool enough to handle, then roll in additional confectioners' sugar.

Yield: About 3 dozen cookies.

Some say that ever 'gainst that season comes
Wherein our Saviour's birth is celebrated,
The bird of dawning singeth all night long;
And then, they say, no spirit can walk abroad;
The nights are wholesome; then no planets strike,
No fairy takes, nor witch hath power to charm,
So hallow'd and so gracious is the time.

Hamlet, Act I, Scene I

Soupirs (Sighs)

3 tablespoons unsalted butter, softened to room temperature
½ cup sugar
3 egg whites
½ teaspoon almond extract
½ cup almonds, finely ground
5 tablespoons all-purpose flour

Preheat oven to 400°F. Lightly butter a baking sheet.

Cream the butter and sugar together until very light and fluffy. Stir in egg whites and almond extract. Stir in ground almonds and flour and blend well. Drop by scant teaspoonfuls onto prepared baking sheet, leaving a space of 2 to 3 inches between each cookie. Bake for 5 to 6 minutes, watching carefully, until edges turn light brown. Cool on wire racks and store in an airtight container.

Yield: about 2 dozen cookies.

Pfeffernuesse (Peppernuts)

This cookie is found throughout Northern Europe at Christmas time. Although popularly associated with Germany, in Sweden they are *pepparanoter*, in Denmark, *pepernoder*, and everywhere, delicious! The dough for this traditional Christmas spice cookie should be allowed to rest in the refrigerator for 1 or 2 days before baking.

3 eggs
1½ cups brown sugar
½ cup honey
¼ cup rum or brandy
1 cup very finely chopped blanched almonds
1 cup chopped white raisins
2 tablespoons candied orange peel, finely chopped
2 tablespoons citron, finely chopped
Grated rind of 1 lemon
3 cups sifted all-purpose flour, approximately
1 teaspoon baking soda
1 teaspoon baking powder
2 teaspoons cinnamon
½ teaspoon black pepper
½ teaspoon cloves
¼ teaspoon nutmeg
¼ teaspoon cardamom
Confectioners' sugar

In a large bowl, beat the eggs with the sugar until mixture is very thick and light in color. Beat in the honey and the brandy. Stir in the almonds, raisins, candied orange peel, citron and lemon rind.

Sift together the flour, baking soda, baking powder, cinnamon, black pepper, cloves, nutmeg, and cardamom. Stir flour and spices gradually into the egg mixture to make a rather firm dough. Remove from bowl onto a floured surface and knead the dough for several minutes until it feels smooth and slightly elastic. Wash and dry the bowl. Rub the inside with butter or vegetable oil. Return the dough to the bowl, cover with plastic wrap and refrigerate for 1 or 2 days.

Preheat oven to 350°F. Grease several cookie sheets with butter or solid vegetable shortening.

Shape cookies into 1-inch balls with your hands and arrange them on the cookie sheets leaving about 1 inch between each cookie. Bake for 20 minutes, until cookies are light brown and hold their shape. The cookies should still be slightly moist inside as they will dry out as they are kept. Let cool slightly on cookie sheets, but roll them in confectioners' sugar while they are still warm. Cool on racks, then store in airtight container. These will keep well for 3 to 4 weeks.

Yield: about 160 cookies.

CINNAMON BUTTER COOKIES

2 sticks unsalted butter, at room temperature
2 cups sugar
1 egg
2¼ cups sifted all-purpose flour
1½ teaspoons cinnamon
Additional butter for cookie sheet

In a large bowl, cream together the butter and 1 cup sugar. Reserve remaining sugar for later. Beat in the egg. Beat in the flour gradually until well blended, then beat in the cinnamon. Refrigerate the dough for 1½ to 2 hours, until firm.

Preheat oven to 350°F.

Lightly butter a cookie sheet. Shape the dough with your hands into balls the size of a walnut and arrange these on the buttered baking sheet about 2 inches apart. Rub the bottom of a drinking glass with butter and dip the glass into the remaining sugar. Use the glass to flatten each ball of dough until it is about ¼ inch thick. Dip the glass in sugar before flattening each cookie. Bake at 350°F. for 15 to 20 minutes until the cookies are golden brown. Let cool for a few minutes on cookie sheet then transfer the cookies onto a wire rack to cool completely.

Keep cookies in tightly covered tin or plastic box for up to 2 weeks.

Yield: 2½ dozen cookies.

Christmas Kisses

2 egg whites, at room temperature
Pinch of salt
1 cup confectioners' sugar
1 cup chopped dates
1 cup chopped walnuts

Preheat oven to 300°F. Lightly grease a baking sheet with butter or vegetable shortening.

Beat the egg whites together with the salt until they form stiff peaks. Gradually beat in the confectioners' sugar. Fold in the dates and nuts. Drop by teaspoonfuls onto prepared baking sheet. Bake 20 to 25 minutes until cookies are just turning color. Cool on wire racks.

Yield: about 2 dozen kisses.

Maple Bars

These are a New England favorite at Christmastime and all through the winter. They are not particularly good keepers, but they don't seem to hang around all that long anyway.

2 sticks unsalted butter, at room temperature
1 cup brown sugar
2 large eggs
1 cup pure maple syrup
2 teaspoons vanilla extract
1½ cups all-purpose flour
1 teaspoon baking powder
1½ cups rolled oats
1 cup coconut flakes
1 cup walnuts, roughly chopped

Preheat oven to 375°F. Grease a 9-by-13-inch baking pan with butter or vegetable shortening.

Cream together the butter and sugar until very light and fluffy. Beat in the eggs one at a time until very frothy and pale lemon-colored. Beat in maple syrup and vanilla extract.

Sift together the flour and baking powder and stir into the liquid mixture. Stir in the rolled oats, coconut, and walnuts. Mix well.

Spread the cookie batter evenly in the prepared baking pan and bake at 375°F. for 25 to 30 minutes, until top is lightly browned. Remove from oven and let cool in pan. Cut into bars or squares.

Yield: about 2 dozen cookies.

It was believed by some nations that if the branches of holly, with their prickly leaves, were cut on Christmas Eve, and hung up in houses and stables, it would capture all the little devils and witches hanging around, or else drive them away, so that they could do no harm. Witches were said to particularly detest holly, because in its name they saw another spelling of the word Holy, and in its thorny foliage and blood-red berries so many Christian suggestions.

Misteltoe is not used in Christian connections on account of its having been the sacred plant of the Druids.

"An old English superstition was that elves and fairies joined in the social gatherings at Christmas, and branches were hung in hall and bower, so that the fays might "hang in each leaf and cling on every bough during that sacred time when spirits have power to harm." These evergreens were to be taken down on Candlemas Eve.

The Housewife
Victorian ladies' periodical

CHRISTMAS
BOX
1882
ST. NICHOLAS
NORTH POLE

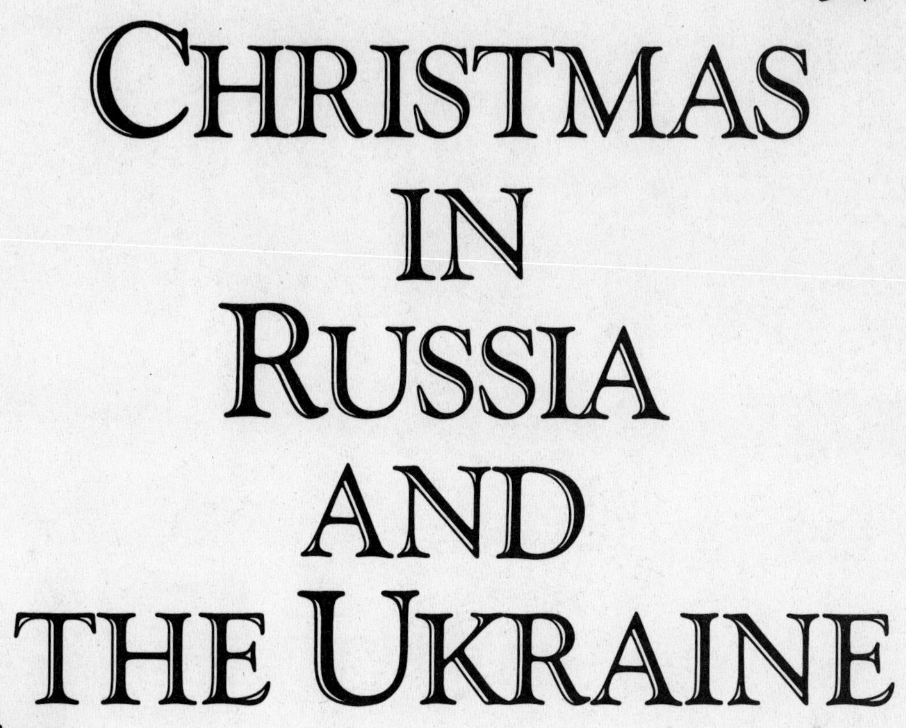

Christmas in Russia and the Ukraine

St. Nicholas was chosen as the patron Saint of Russia because, according to tradition, the eleventh-century prince Vladimir the Great, having traveled to Constantinople to be baptized, returned with stories of the miracles worked by Bishop Nicholas of Myra. Since that time, many Russian Orthodox churches have been dedicated to him, and Nicholas remains one of the most common names for Russian boys. St. Nicholas's feast day was devoutly observed for many centuries, though since the Russian revolution many religious customs have been suppressed. Nevertheless, traditional carols, known as *kolyadki*, are still sung, children are still told about a Santa Claus-like figure now called Grandfather Frost, and people still decorate their "New Year trees."

Before the revolution, Christmas gifts for children were brought by Babouschka, an old woman who, like Befana in Italy, is said to have failed to join the three wise men on their quest and now wanders the countryside looking for the Infant Jesus.

Decorations for Christmas trees were a common tradition in nineteenth-century Russia, though for the peasants most were home-made, often consisting of apples, walnuts, and tangerines put up with string, and dolls made of dried fruit and candy.

Old superstitions often endured, and as a result Christmas was considered the season of fortune-telling. Omens were seen everywhere: A frost indicated an excellent grain harvest the following year, starry skies augured well for peas, and cloudy skies meant the cows would be productive. It was also the traditional time for free Russian servants to renew their agreements with their masters or else move on—a difficult decision that was rarely made without recourse to a holiday drink or two.

In Russia as in many eastern European countries, Christmas Eve, while always a joyous and festive occasion, is still considered part of the Advent season and thus part

of the meatless fast season associated with it. As a result Christmas Eve dinner often features fish and other meatless and dairy-free delicacies like borscht, grain-stuffed cabbage leaves, and a special porridge called *kutya*. Traditionally at this meal the floor and table were strewn with hay to commemorate the manger in which Christ was born, and the meal itself was not to begin until a child in the family had spied the first star of evening.

Ukrainians and many other Slavic people follow the Julian calendar, and so for them Christmas falls on January 6. Midnight Mass is traditional, as is the caroling of the *kolyadniky*, singers who travel from house to house entertaining the residents with songs about the birth of Christ and hoping for gifts.

The most important food associated with Christmas in Russia and other Eastern European countries is kutya, the original version of which was made with wheatberries, poppy seeds, and honey. An ancient ritual food whose origin is lost in the mists of time, it is always served on Christmas Eve and, since the fragrance of the honey in the kutya was thought to be the only sustenance the soul needed on its journey, it was also served at funerals. In some places it was eaten right at the grave site, with every alternate spoonful being tossed onto the coffin.

On Christmas Eve the kutya, eaten from a common dish symbolizing unity, helps to recall departed ancestors. The grain of which it is made is emblematic of hope and immortality, and the sweet, rich taste of the honey and poppy seeds are said to ensure happiness, success, and an untroubled rest. In many families kutya is served on a bed of hay, and in some areas it is customary to fling a spoonful of kutya up to the ceiling: If it sticks, bees will swarm and the harvest will be plentiful; if not, then someone will have a mess in his hair.

TRADITIONAL KUTYA

1 cup whole wheatberries
½ teaspoon salt
1 cup honey
1 cup ground poppy seeds

Soak the wheatberries to cover overnight. Drain the wheatberries and cook in 4 cups water and the ½ teaspoon salt, until tender. This will take about 2 hours.

In a small saucepan, heat the honey over low heat and stir in the ground poppy seeds.

When the wheatberries have cooked remove them to a large bowl. Stir in honey and poppy seeds together with ½ to ¾ cup of boiling water. The kutya should have a slightly soupy consistency.

Yield: 6 servings.

UKRAINIAN CHRISTMAS KALACH

This braided Christmas loaf is traditional Christmas fare in all Ukrainian families. It is a lovely festive bread.

1½ cups milk
⅓ cup flour
2 teaspoons sugar
4 packages active dry yeast
½ cup warm water
4 egg yolks
4 whole eggs
1 teaspoon salt
1 cup sugar
1 cup melted butter
2 teaspoons vanilla extract
7½ to 8 cups sifted all-purpose flour
1 egg beaten with 1 tablespoon water
½ cup poppy seeds

In a saucepan, bring the milk to a boil and immediately remove from heat. Gradually stir the milk into ⅓ cup flour, stirring constantly until the mixture is smooth.

Dissolve sugar and yeast in ½ cup of warm water and let stand until it becomes frothy. Combine with the milk and flour mixture. Cover and let stand in a warm place for about 1 hour to make a sponge.

Beat the egg yolks together with the eggs. Beat in the salt and gradually beat in the sugar until mixture is very light and frothy. Beat in the butter and vanilla extract. Combine with the sponge and mix well.

Stir in enough flour to make a soft but workable dough and knead it for about 10 minutes until it is very smooth and elastic. Cover and let rise in a warm place until double in bulk, about 1½ to 2 hours.

Punch down the dough, knead for about 5 minutes, cover, and let rise again until double in bulk, 1 to 1½ hours.

Remove the dough to a lightly floured surface and divide into three parts. Roll each piece of dough into a long roll 1 to 1½-inches thick. Braid the rolls together and join the ends to form a ring. Transfer to a large buttered baking sheet, cover, and let rise for 1 hour, or until double in bulk.

Preheat oven to 375°F.

Brush the loaf with the beaten egg and sprinkle with poppy seeds. Bake for 10 minutes and lower temperature to 325°F. Bake for 30 minutes, and lower temperature to 275°F. Bake 20 minutes longer. Remove and let cool before serving.

Yield: 1 braided kalach.

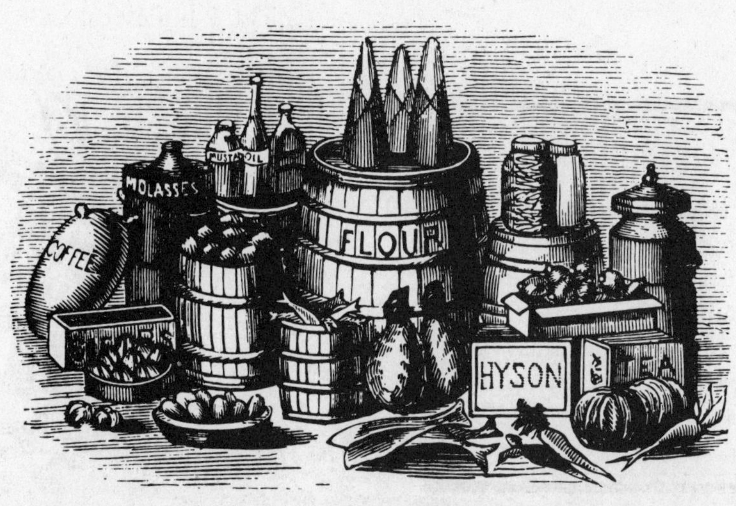

MEDIVNYK (UKRAINIAN HONEY LOAF)

The Ukraine is famous for its honey, and various honey cakes and pastries are traditional at Christmas. Buckwheat honey is always the honey of choice. The *medivnyk*, which takes its name from the Ukrainian word for honey, is the traditional Christmas honey cake. It should be allowed to stand and ripen for a few days before serving.

1 cup buckwheat or other dark honey
1 teaspoon cinnamon
½ teaspoon cloves
½ teaspoon grated nutmeg
1 cup seedless raisins
½ cup currants
½ cup pitted dates, chopped
1 cup walnuts, chopped
1 stick unsalted butter, softened to room temperature
1 cup brown sugar
4 eggs, separated
¼ cup strong coffee
3 cups sifted all-purpose flour
2 teaspoons baking soda
1 teaspoon baking powder
¼ teaspoon salt

In a saucepan, combine honey, cinnamon, cloves, and nutmeg. Bring to a boil, remove from heat, and allow to cool.

In a large bowl, combine raisins, currants, dates, and walnuts. Sprinkle with 2 tablespoons of flour and mix well.

Cream butter and sugar together until light and fluffy. Beat in egg yolks one at a time until mixture is very light and frothy. Beat in coffee and stir in honey mixture.

Preheat oven to 325°F. Grease two 8-inch loaf pans with butter and line with baking parchment.

Sift the remaining flour with the baking soda, baking powder, and salt. Stir the flour into the honey fruit mixture to make a batter. Beat the egg whites until they form stiff peaks and fold them into the batter. Spoon the batter into the prepared loaf pans and bake for about 2 hours, or until a cake tester comes out clean. Turn out of pans, remove parchment, and let cool. Wrap and let stand a few days before serving.

Yield: 2 honey cakes.

In the town of Bethlehem, Christmas is celebrated on three different dates each year: December 25, the traditional date for most Christians, January 18, for members of the Armenian Church, and January 6 for followers of the Greek Orthodox tradition.

RICE AND RAISIN KUTYA

1 cup long-grain rice
¼ teaspoon salt
3 tablespoons toasted almonds, chopped
¼ cup golden raisins
1 cup honey
1 cup water

Place the rice and salt together with 2½ cups water into a saucepan. Bring to a boil, stir, cover, and reduce heat to low. Simmer for 20 minutes or until all the liquid is absorbed. Remove to a large bowl and mix together with the raisins.

Heat the honey and water in a saucepan until all the honey has dissolved. Stir well and pour into a small pitcher. Serve with kutya. A small amount of honeyed water is poured over a serving of kutya.

Yield: 6 servings.

KISSEL

This is a simple but very lovely Russian dessert. Its bright red color makes it particularly appealing at Christmastime.

1 pound cranberries
2 cups water
1 cup sugar
2 tablespoons cornstarch
2 tablespoons orange juice

In a large saucepan, simmer the cranberries together with the water and sugar until the cranberries pop, about 15 minutes. Put through a food mill to purée. Strain through a fine sieve to remove the seeds if you wish. Return the cranberry purée to the saucepan. Mix cornstarch and orange juice together and stir into the cranberry purée. Cook over low heat, stirring, for about 5 minutes, until thickened. Serve chilled with heavy cream.

Yield: 6 to 8 servings.

Christmas in Scandinavia

Scandinavian Christmas, with its snow-bound landscapes, rustic settings, and snug homes complete with burning Yule logs, hearty toasts, and wonderful meals, probably comes close to embodying the American ideal of holiday ambience. Though the Scandinavian countries have histories and customs that are in many ways distinct, when it comes to Christmas, many of those distinctions tend to blur and the customs to overlap.

Yuletide, the "turning of the sun" or the winter solstice, has always been considered a portentous time in Scandinavia, a time when the fortunes of the coming year are determined, and a time when the dead are thought to walk the earth. In fact, Christmas Eve was long considered a dangerous time to sleep alone, and on that one night the entire extended family, master and servant alike, slept together on freshly spread straw.

Scandinavia's position in the far northern latitudes ensures that winters there are both dark and cold, and so it is not surprising that many of the Yule traditions are concerned with light and warmth. It is from Scandinavia that many of the traditions surrounding the Yule log come. Originally the Yule log was an entire tree, carefully selected and brought into the house with great ceremony, then arranged with just the butt end in the hearth while the rest of the log stuck out into the room. The log was slowly fed into the fire as it was consumed, and the entire process was carefully timed to last for the length of the Yule season. Another custom, the Julebaal, or Christmas fire, is traditionally lit outdoors but positioned so that it can be seen from inside the house.

In Norway candles are often lit at Christmastime for each member of the family, and the light from these candles is thought to bring special fortune to anyone on whom it shines.

The basic shape of a pretzel is the sign of the baker in Scandinavia. The pretzel shape has special significance at Christmastime, since it is derived from an ancient calendar symbol used to mark the winter solstice. Originally it was a circle (representing the orbit of the sun) with a dot in the center representing the earth. Represented in the form of a cookie, the dot inevitably became a cross. Later, when the design was contrived with a single piece of rolled dough, the design became yet further stylized and assumed the shape we know today.

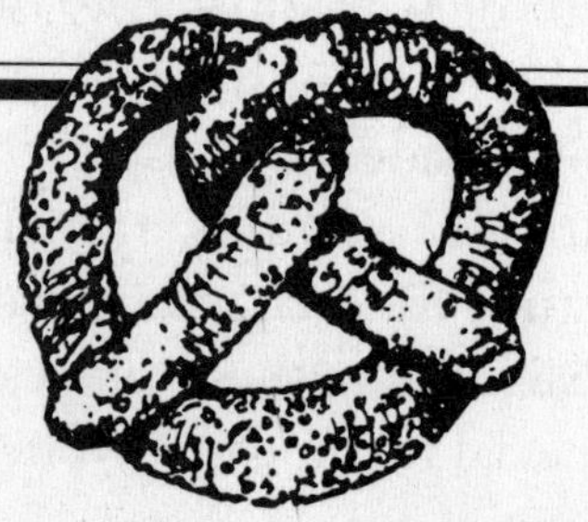

In Sweden, the thousand-year-old tradition, traceable back to King Canute (or Knute) who first declared it so, is that Christmas lasts a month, that is to say that the Yule celebrations begin with the feast of St. Lucia on December 13, and last until January 13 or Tjugondag Knut.

It is also a Swedish tradition that on the morning of December 13, the eldest daughter of the family, dressed as St. Lucia with a headdress of lighted candles, brings coffee and special Christmas buns called *lussekatter* to the bed of each family member. How this third-century Sicilian saint became a Scandinavian heroine is unclear. Some say that she once brought food to the hungry people of one of Sweden's provinces. Others say that early missionaries brought tales of her deeds to the North. In any case it seems that having refused a non-Christian suitor, she was denounced for being a Christian, and tortured to death. Known as the Queen of Light and always pictured wearing a crown of candles, she is a figure of endless fascination for the Swedes.

The slaughtering of animals, especially the "Christmas pig," is delayed until just before the holiday season begins, and on Christmas day a bowl of porridge is left in the hayloft of the barn as a treat for the *nisse*, or barn elf, a mischievous creature somewhere between an elf and a leprechaun, who must be assuaged to avoid no end of small troubles in the coming year.

St. Nicholas and Santa Claus have become popular all over Scandinavia, but the older gift-giving figure in Norway is *Julesvenn*, or "Yule man," who in the past hid a barley straw in the house to be eagerly sought and found by the children of the family on Christmas morning. In Sweden it is Jultomten who distributes the gifts, though clearly he is more like a household or guardian spirit—not unrelated to the gnomelike nisse.

St. Stephen was one of the first missionaries to reach Sweden (in A.D. 1050) and as a result his feast day, December 26, is especially honored there and is known as the second day of Christmas. It is said that because he is the patron saint of animals, all farm animals are given extra food on his day. That may be true, but the custom of giving extra food to domestic beasts at Yuletide goes back well before the Christian era and is honored in nearly every part of the world.

On Twelfth Night, especially in rural areas, it is common for young people to dress up in extravagant costumes carrying candle "stars" on the ends of long poles. They are known as "star boys" and they travel from house to house, singing hymns and carols, especially those that relate to the Epiphany.

The Christmas customs in Denmark,

though distinguished in small ways that reflect that national identity, are not very different from those of the other Scandinavian countries. But it was the Danish national treasure, Hans Christian Andersen, whose Christmas classics, "The Fir Tree" and "The Little Match Girl," were, almost as much as Charles Dickens's *A Christmas Carol*, responsible for creating the image of Christmas that has come to be shared by nearly every Christian nation in the world.

In Scandinavia, and wherever in the world Scandinavians have settled, it is a common practice to fasten a sheaf of grain and perhaps a bit of suet to a pole to provide a Christmas feast for the birds. Many a Scandinavian peasant has refused to sit down to his Christmas meal until he knows that the birds have been thus provided for.

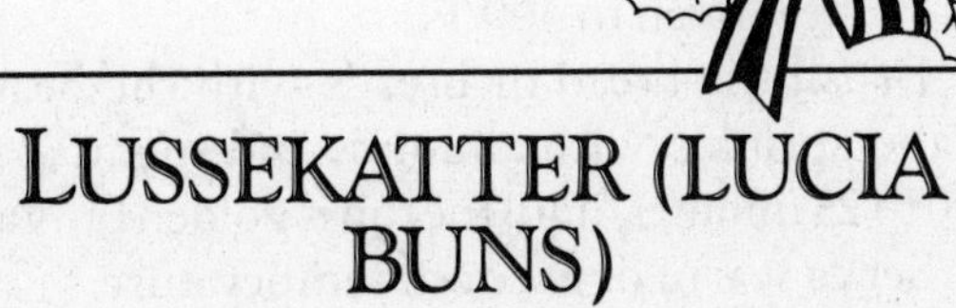

LUSSEKATTER (LUCIA BUNS)

The young lady selected to play the role of St. Lucia carries a tray of lussekatter and coffee to the members of the family. Lussekatter are Lucia "cats," the reference being the catlike raisin eyes at the top of these buns.

½ teaspoon dried saffron
2 packages active dry yeast
¼ cup warm water
1 cup milk
½ cup sugar
1 stick unsalted butter
½ teaspoon salt
1 egg
½ cup currants
¼ cup candied orange peel
¼ cup candied lemon peel
4 cups sifted all-purpose flour
½ cup raisins
1 egg yolk beaten with 2 tablespoons water

Steep the saffron in about 3 tablespoons boiling water for 2 hours. In a large mixing bowl, sprinkle the yeast into ¼ cup warm water along with a pinch of sugar. Let stand about 10 minutes until foamy.

Bring the milk almost to a boil and remove from heat. Combine the milk with the sugar, butter, and salt. Stir until the sugar has dissolved and the butter has completely melted. Add the strained saffron water and let stand until milk has cooled to lukewarm. Pour the milk into the bowl with the yeast mixture. Beat the egg and stir into the milk.

Combine the currants, candied orange peel, and lemon peel together with 2 tablespoons flour and mix well to coat every piece. Set aside.

Gradually stir the flour into the milk mixture to make soft but workable dough. Add the currants and candied peels. Remove dough to a lightly floured surface and knead for 10 minutes, until dough is smooth and elastic. Add more flour as needed. Place the dough in a greased bowl, cover, and let rise in a warm place until doubled in bulk, 1½ to 2 hours.

Lightly grease a baking sheet with butter or vegetable shortening.

Punch the dough down and knead briefly, about 5 minutes. Divide the dough into 24 pieces and shape into round buns. Press 2 raisins into each bun. Arrange the buns on prepared baking sheets. Brush tops with egg yolk beaten with water. Cover loosely with a towel and let rise for 30 minutes.

Preheat oven to 400°F.

Bake for 15 minutes and reduce oven temperature to 350°F. Bake 30 minutes longer, or until golden brown.

Yield: 2 dozen buns.

KRINGLE

This Danish Advent bread is shaped in the form of a pretzel. It is a slightly sweet bread, that can be served like a coffee cake. In fact, in Denmark this type of yeast cake is called a coffee bread. This is a very impressive looking bread, utterly delicious, and not at all difficult to make. It is at its best when eaten the same day it is baked.

The cake:

2 packages active dry yeast
½ cup warm milk
4 tablespoons sugar
1 stick plus 4 tablespoons unsalted butter, at room temperature
2 large eggs
1 teaspoon cardamom
½ teaspoon salt
4 to 5 cups all-purpose flour

The filling:

1 stick unsalted butter, at room temperature
1 cup sugar
1½ teaspoons cinnamon

The topping:

1 egg, well beaten
1 cup almonds, coarsely chopped
12 sugar cubes, coarsely chopped

Sprinkle yeast into the warm milk along with a pinch of sugar. Let stand for 10 minutes until yeast is dissolved and starts to foam. Cream butter and sugar together, beat in the eggs, stir in yeast mixture and blend well. Stir in cardamom and salt, then gradually stir in enough flour to make a soft but workable dough. Remove to a lightly floured surface and knead for about 10 minutes until the dough is smooth and elastic. Place the dough in a greased bowl, cover and let stand for about 2 hours, or until the dough has doubled in bulk.

Prepare the filling. Mix butter, sugar, and cinnamon together. Grease a large baking sheet and line with baking parchment.

Roll the dough on a lightly floured surface into a long strip that is about 5 inches wide. If you prefer, you can roll out two strips, 5 inches wide, for two smaller breads. Spread the filling down the center of the strip, and fold the two edges over the center to enclose the filling. Carefully transfer the strip or strips of dough onto the prepared baking sheet and arrange the dough in the shape of a large pretzel. Jane Grigson's very helpful hint is to think of the dough as folding your arms across, so that your hands touch the opposite shoulders. That is the shape you want. Cover the dough loosely with a towel and let rest in a warm place for 30 minutes.

Preheat oven to 400°F.

Brush the bread or breads with the beaten egg and sprinkle with almonds and sugar. Bake for 20 to 25 minutes, until the top is golden brown.

Serve warm or at room temperature.

Yield: 1 large or 2 smaller Kringle breads.

GLÖGG (MULLED WINE)

Glögg means "glow" in Swedish, and a good glögg glows twice, once when it is being made in the traditional manner with burning sugar infused into the drink and the second time when it is consumed. The warming cheery glow one gets from drinking glögg can make one grateful for the coming of winter.

3 bottles red Bordeaux wine
1 large orange, sliced into rounds
12 whole cloves
12 cardamom seeds
1 cinnamon stick
8 dried figs
2 cups blanched whole almonds
2 cups seedless raisins
2 bottles aquavit
1 pound sugar cubes

Pour the wine into a large enameled or stainless steel saucepan. Stick the cloves into the orange slices and add to the wine. Add cardamom, cinnamon, and figs. Cook over low heat until just hot but not boiling. Mix almonds and raisins together in a small bowl and reserve. Pour the wine into a large ceramic or silver punch bowl. (A less elegant approach, but perfectly practical if you don't own such a bowl, is to keep the wine in its pot. Serve the punch family style, from the kitchen.)

Heat the aquavit in another enameled saucepan until hot but not boiling. Place the sugar cubes in a stainless steel sieve with a long handle. Hold the sieve directly over the wine. Pour a little hot aquavit over the sugar cubes and ignite them. Continue to pour aquavit over the sugar to keep it burning until all the sugar has melted into the wine.

To serve, place a few almonds and raisins in the bottom of each punch cup. Ladle hot glögg over the raisins and nuts.

Yield: 30 to 40 servings

NOTE: Another way to melt the sugar is to place the sugar cubes directly in the bottom of a heavy ceramic or silver punch bowl. Moisten the sugar with hot aquavit and ignite. Continue pouring hot aquavit over the burning sugar cubes then pour into the hot wine.

When they saw the star, they rejoiced with exceeding great joy.

And when they were come into the house, they saw the young child with Mary his mother, and fell down, and worshiped him . . . they presented unto him gifts; gold, and frankincense, and myrrh.

Matthew 2:10–11

Herring Salad

Herring salad is part of the Christmas table throughout most of Scandinavia. Make this dish two or three days before you wish to serve it. Herring salad is a great addition to the buffet table for a large party.

3 salt herrings
1½ to 2 cups diced cooked veal, lamb, beef, or pork
1½ cups cooked beets (canned are okay), diced
2 Granny Smith apples, peeled, cored, and diced
3 to 4 large boiled potatoes, skinned and diced
2 dill pickles, diced
1 small red onion, finely chopped
¼ cup red wine vinegar
3 tablespoons olive oil
3 tablespoons sugar
Freshly ground black pepper
4 hard-boiled eggs, peeled and chopped
½ cup heavy cream
½ cup sour cream

Soak the herrings in cold water to cover for at least 12 hours. Change the water several times.

Remove and discard the heads and fillet the herrings. Wash and pat dry on paper towels. Cut herring fillets into bite-size pieces and put them in a large bowl. Add the meat, beets, apples, potatoes, pickles, and onion. Mix all these ingredients together.

Mix vinegar, oil, sugar, and freshly ground black pepper to taste together and pour over the salad ingredients. Garnish with chopped hard-boiled eggs. Beat the heavy cream until stiff and fold into sour cream. Serve in a separate bowl as garnish for the herring salad.

Yield: 10 to 12 servings.

Swedish Christmas Spareribs

5 pounds spareribs
1 tablespoon salt
1 teaspoon freshly ground black pepper
1 tablespoon ginger
1 tablespoon dry mustard

In a very large pot bring the spareribs and enough water to cover to a boil. Reduce heat and simmer for 20 minutes. Drain the spareribs.

Preheat oven to 325°F.

Mix together the salt, freshly ground black pepper, ginger, and mustard. Rub into the spareribs. Place the ribs on a rack in a roasting pan. Pour 2 cups water into the bottom of the roasting pan. Bake for 1½ hours, until ribs are very tender.

Yield: 6 to 8 servings.

Swedish Red Cabbage Salad

1 cup applesauce
1 to 2 tablespoons prepared horseradish
1 small head red cabbage (about 1 pound)
Salt to taste
Freshly ground black pepper to taste

Shred the cabbage and place in a salad bowl. Mix together the applesauce and horseradish. Combine with shredded cabbage and mix well. Season with salt and pepper to taste. Chill before serving. (This can be made a day ahead.)

Yield: 6 servings.

RIS À L'AMANDE (CHRISTMAS RICE PUDDING)

3¾ cups milk
1 cup long-grain rice
⅓ cup sugar
½ cup blanched almonds, chopped
½ cup sweet sherry
½ teaspoon cinnamon
1½ teaspoons vanilla extract
1 cup heavy cream
Raspberry or strawberry preserves

In a large heavy enameled pot, bring the milk to a boil. Reduce heat and add the rice and sugar. Simmer uncovered for 25 minutes or until the rice is tender but not mushy. Remove from heat and let cool. Stir in almonds, sherry, cinnamon, and vanilla extract.

Beat the heavy cream until stiff and fold into the cool rice mixture. Chill well before serving. Serve in glass bowls with a dollop of raspberry or strawberry preserves on top.

Yield: 8 to 10 servings.

Rice Porridge For Christmas Eve

In Norway and Denmark a rice porridge is traditional Christmas fare. It is sprinkled with cinnamon and hidden in it are an almond and a raisin. It is said that whoever finds the almond will have good luck (and will be the next to get married!) and whoever finds the raisin is the one who must do the dishes (unless he or she is clever enough to swallow it and say nothing!).

CHRISTMAS
IN
SPAIN
AND
PORTUGAL

Known as *Nochebuena*, or the Good Night, Christmas Eve in Spain is first and foremost a time of family reunion, and though friends may be much beloved, it is primarily family members who gather to rejoice and feast around the *nacimientos*, manger scenes, and illuminated shrines, that are set up in nearly every home. The special treat at Christmas time is the *turron*, a kind of almond candy that is said to have been introduced (or at least inspired) by sacrificial cakes made by the Carthaginians many centuries ago.

The Virgin Mary is the patron saint of Spain, and so it is the feast of the Immaculate Conception on December 8 that starts off the Christmas season there. In front of Seville's great Gothic cathedral the ceremony known as *los Seises*, or the "dance of the Six," is performed every year at this time, as well as on Easter and on Corpus Christi. Oddly, the rite is now performed by not six but ten young boys, each carefully trained under ecclesiastical auspices and each handsomely done up in lavish costume. The dance itself is a series of solemn ritual signs and movements that recall to some visitors the geisha dances of Japan. Every moment and gesture is said to have special significance, and the overall effect is said to be stunningly moving and beautiful.

The Magi are particularly beloved figures in Spain, and it is believed that each year they travel through the country recapitulating their journey to Bethlehem. In the past it was customary in Spain, and Portugal as well, for townsfolk to go out looking for them on Epiphany Eve in a great festive procession, complete with musical instruments to welcome the caravan and with food and treats to give them as gifts. Traditionally the search was in vain, and the children, disappointed, were allowed to have the treats. Then one of the adults would announce that the wise men were at the church and everyone would hurry there to see the elaborate nacimiento that had been prepared there. After singing many traditional carols, the children would be sent to

bed, but not before they filled their shoes with straw in the hopes of finding yet more treats there in the morning.

On December 28, the Feast of the Holy Innocents, the boys of a town will light bonfires and elect a mayor who may order the citizens to perform small civic chores like cleaning the streets. Failure to comply will result in a fine which is used to pay for the costs of the Holy Innocents celebration.

On Christmas Day there are feasts and much gift giving and also the custom of the Urn of Fate. In other European countries the Urn of Fate is also a gift-giving ritual—a kind of grab bag wherein gifts placed in a large bowl are drawn out blindly. In Spain, however, the practice has evolved into a sort of matchmaking event. Everyone's name is written on cards that are then thrown in the urn. The cards are drawn out two at a time and the resulting pairs are expected to have a special friendship in the ensuing year. Naturally, a certain amount of cheating is not unexpected so that certain promising couples can have a chance to get together.

Another common feature of any feast day in Spain, but especially Christmas, is the parades of *gigantes*, immense wood or papier-mâché puppets that are animated by a man hiding inside. Made to represent kings and queens and historical and mythological figures, they dance and whirl about, lending a colorful and fantastical air to the riotous celebrations, which climax on Christmas Eve with the pealing of the church bells and traditional midnight Mass, followed by the Christmas feast for which everyone has been waiting.

In Portugal the Christmas banquet, called *consoada*, is also held in the early morning hours of Christmas Day, often as the Yule log, or *fogueira da consoda*, burns in the hearth. Places are set at the table for *alminhas a penar*, or souls of the dead, and in some areas crumbs are left for them on the hearth. This last custom harks back to a very old tradition of trusting the care of seeds to the dead in the hope that they will provide an abundant harvest in the coming year.

BESUGO A LA MADRILENA (BAKED WHOLE PORGY)

A whole fish such as a porgy baked in white wine and tomato sauce is a traditional part of the Christmas Eve dinner.

4 porgies, each about ¾-pound, or 1 large porgy, about 4 pounds, cleaned but with heads on
1 lemon, very thinly sliced
Juice of 1 lemon
4 tablespoons olive oil
1 small onion, finely chopped
¾ cup tomato sauce
1 bay leaf
1 cup dry white wine
½ teaspoon salt
Freshly ground black pepper
3 garlic cloves, put through garlic press
¼ cup parsley, finely minced

Preheat oven to 350°F.

Make diagonal cuts about 1 inch apart on both sides of each fish. Insert a lemon slice in each. Sprinkle the fish with lemon juice.

In a skillet, heat 2 tablespoons of the olive oil and sauté the onion for 10 to 15 minutes until it is wilted. Add the tomato sauce, bay leaf, and ½ cup of wine. Simmer for 15 to 20 minutes.

Select a shallow ovenproof casserole that is large enough to hold the fish in one layer. Brush the bottom with 1 tablespoon of the olive oil. Arrange the fish, brush them with the remaining olive oil, and sprinkle with salt and freshly ground black pepper. Add the remaining ½ glass of white wine and spoon the tomato sauce over the fish. Place in oven and bake for 10 minutes.

Mix together the garlic and parsley and sprinkle over the fish. Bake for 45 minutes, until the fish is done.

Yield: 4 servings.

VARIATION: Some recipes call for the addition of bread crumbs to garlic and parsley. And some cooks add peeled, sliced potatoes for the final 30 minutes of cooking.

SOPA DE ALMENDRES (ALMOND SOUP)

Almonds are a recurring theme in Spain's Christmas celebrations.

3 slices stale white bread, crusts removed
1⅓ cups blanched almonds
4 cloves garlic
1 teaspoon olive oil
4 teaspoons wine vinegar
8 cups ice water
Seedless white grapes

In a small bowl, soak the bread in cold water to cover. Place the almonds, garlic, and salt into the bowl of a food processor and process to a fine paste. Squeeze the bread to remove most of the water and add it to the almond mixture. With the food processor on, add the olive oil in a stream, then add the vinegar.

Remove the mixture to a large bowl and gradually whisk in the ice water. Taste for seasoning and add more salt if necessary. Garnish each serving with 4 seedless grapes, cut in half.

Yield: 6 to 8 servings.

And it came to pass in those days, that there went out a decree from Caesar Augustus, that all the world should be taxed. . . .

And all went to be taxed, every one into his own city.

And Joseph also went up from Galilee, out of the city of Nazareth, into Judea, unto the city of David, which is called Bethlehem (because he was of the house and lineage of David).

To be taxed with Mary his espoused wife, being great with child.

And so it was, that, while they were there, the days were accomplished that she should be delivered. And she brought forth her firstborn son, and wrapped him in swaddling clothes and laid him in a manger; because there was no room for them in the inn.

And there were in the same country shepherds abiding in the field, keeping watch over their flocks by night.

And, lo, the Angel of the Lord came upon them, and the glory of the Lord shone round about them; and they were sore afraid.

And the angel said unto them, Fear not, for behold, I bring you good tidings of great joy, which shall be to all people.

For unto you is born this day in the city of David a Savior, which is Christ the Lord.

And this shall be a sign unto you; Ye shall find the babe wrapped in swaddling clothes, lying in a manger.

And suddenly there was with the Angel a multitude of heavenly host praising God, and saying.

Glory to God in the highest, and on earth peace, good will toward men.

Luke 2:1–4

COCHINILLO ASADO (ROAST SUCKLING PIG)

Roast suckling pig is a holiday food in many countries and cultures. It is often served at Christmastime in Spain, and this recipe is one of the best for this most luscious of delicacies.

1 7- or 8-pound suckling pig
Salt
Freshly ground black pepper
3 large onions, finely chopped
4 cloves garlic, finely chopped
2 cups fresh parsley, finely chopped
1 teaspoon thyme
1 teaspoon marjoram
2 cups dry white wine
Olive oil

Preheat oven to 350°F.

Wash the pig inside and out and pat it dry. Pierce the skin with the tines of a fork in several places. Rub inside and out with salt and freshly ground black pepper. Tie the front legs forward and tie the back legs under the body. Mix together the onions, garlic, parsley, thyme, and marjoram. Stuff this into the cavity of the pig. Place on a rack in a roasting pan. Pour 2 cups of wine and 2 cups of water into the bottom of the roasting pan. Roast in a preheated 350°F. oven, allowing 30 minutes per pound. Baste frequently with the pan juice and add more wine or water if necessary. Stop basting for the last 30 minutes of roasting and brush the pig all over with olive oil to brown. Remove the pig and set aside. Skim the fat from the pan juices, season to taste with salt and pepper, and serve in a gravy boat.

Yield: 6 to 8 servings.

ROSCON DE REYES (THREE KINGS BREAD)

The day of the Three Kings on January 6 (Epiphany) is the major winter holiday in Spain. The Three Wise Men (the kings) are said to have journeyed to Spain on camels and brought gifts for all Spanish children. And on this day gifts are still exchanged. It is customary to hide a coin in the roscon and the person who finds it will have good luck in the coming year.

2 packages active dry yeast
½ cup warm water
¾ cup milk
1 stick unsalted butter
½ cup sugar
½ teaspoon salt
Grated rind of 1 lemon
3 eggs
5 cups sifted all-purpose flour
1 cup mixed candied fruits, coarsely chopped
1 cup blanched almonds, coarsely chopped
¼ cup milk
¼ cup sugar

Sprinkle the yeast over the warm water along with a pinch of sugar. Let stand for 5 to 10 mintues until mixture is frothy. Heat the milk until almost boiling and put it in a bowl together with the butter. Stir to mix well. Stir in sugar, salt, and grated lemon rind. Beat the eggs and stir into the milk. Stir in yeast mixture. Gradually stir in the flour to make a workable dough.

Remove the dough to a lightly floured surface and knead for about 10 minutes, until dough is smooth and elastic.

Place the dough in a greased bowl, cover, and let stand in a warm place until double in bulk, 1½ to 2 hours.

Lightly grease a baking sheet with butter or vegetable shortening.

Punch down the dough, knead briefly, mixing in the candied fruit and almonds. Tuck a coin into the dough. Shape into a ring and arrange on prepared baking sheet. Cover loosely with a towel and let rise until double in bulk, about 1 hour.

Preheat oven to 350°F.

Bake for about 1 hour, until golden brown and hollow-sounding when tapped on bottom. Brush with milk and sprinkle with sugar for the last 5 minutes of baking.

Yield: 1 bread.

CHRISTMAS
IN
THE
UNITED STATES

It is thought that the very first Christmas celebrated in the New World occurred when Columbus's ship, the *Santa Maria*, struck a sandbar on Christmas Day, 1492. Rescued and brought to shore by natives of the island later known as Santo Domingo, he celebrated the feast of the Nativity by naming the village he founded La Navidad, "the Nativity."

But Christmas did not get off to a very good start in the New World, since the Puritans frowned on any and all celebrations. In New England in 1659, celebrating Christmas was forbidden by a law that read: "Anybody who is found observing, by abstinence from labor, feasting, or any other way, any such days as Christmas Day, shall pay for every such offense five shillings."

Of course, all that changed with the great influx of European immigrants who reached our shores in the eighteenth and ninteenth centuries. The United States is one of the great melting pots of the world, and it follows that Christmas is celebrated in widely different styles among Christian Americans and even among non-Christians who often enter gleefully into a kind of secularized spirit of the season. Most Christmas traditions in the United States can be traced to the folkways and customs of the homelands of those who have come here. Nevertheless if America lacks a large number of truly distinctive Christmas traditions, it has certainly demonstrated a flair for synthesizing the diverse traditions of the many ethnic groups that live here. It was an American, a New York clergyman named Clement C. Moore, who by writing "A Visit from St. Nicholas" virtually defined the modern notion of Santa Claus as a jolly, bearded fat man with eight reindeer to pull his sleigh. And of course it was the drawings of the famous political cartoonist, Thomas Nast, which brought that notion visually alive.

George Washington

It is no doubt well known to every schoolchild in the United States that the celebration of Christmas played an oblique though important role in the liberation of the colonies from the tyranny of George III. Knowing that the English troops and Hessian mercenaries would not be up to their usual fighting muster because of the day's celebrations, George Washington chose to cross the Delaware on Christmas Day, 1776, thereby successfully surprising and surrounding his unprepared enemy at Trenton, New Jersey.

Two particular elements of the traditional European Christmas to which Americans have taken with special vigor are gift giving, and decorating the Christmas tree.

Gift giving at Christmastime has become an almost obsessive preoccupation for Americans, with special merchandizing promotions beginning now early in November and reaching a peak in the last weeks before the holiday itself. No matter how often or earnestly the "commercialization of Christmas" is decried, it remains a phenomenon upon which large parts of the American economy are largely dependent.

The idea of a lighted and decorated Christmas tree, which was brought to the New World by German settlers, has become perhaps the most central emblem of the season's festivities, even in desert areas where traditional evergreen trees are not readily available. The White House always has an official Christmas tree, and the lighting of the tree in Rockefeller Center is an event televised live all over the nation.

"A Snow Scene on Boston Common."
From *Ballou's Pictorial Drawingroom Companion*, 1856.

The Moravians, an early sect of German Protestants, migrated to America in the eighteenth century. They celebrated Christmas with a love feast that included reading the scriptures, eating delicious cakes, and listening to sacred music.

MORAVIAN LOVE FEAST BUNS

The Moravian candlelight Christmas Eve service, affectionately called a love feast, always featured platters of these delicious sweet buns for the congregation to enjoy with a cup of coffee while they listened to the singing of the choir.

2 cups warm water
1 tablespoon active dry yeast
1 cup sugar
1 large egg
4 tablespoons unsalted butter, softened to room temperature
½ teaspoon salt
¼ cup mashed potatoes
7 to 8 cups all-purpose flour
Melted butter or heavy cream for glazing

Dissolve the yeast in the warm water. Beat sugar, egg, and butter together. Stir in salt and mashed potatoes. Stir in yeast water. Stir in 3 cups of flour and mix until smooth. Add enough more flour to make a smooth, workable dough. Spread some flour on a work surface and knead for 5 to 10 minutes until very smooth and satiny. Place in a greased bowl and cover with a towel. Let stand in a warm place until dough doubles in bulk, about 1½ hours.

Grease several cookie sheets with butter or vegetable shortening.

Punch down dough and knead briefly. Divide dough into four parts and divide each part into 5 rolls. Arrange rolls about 1 inch apart on prepared cookie sheets. Cover with a towel and let rise again until double in size, about 45 minutes.

Preheat oven to 400°F.

Bake for 20 minutes, until rolls are golden brown. Brush hot rolls with melted butter or heavy cream. Serve warm or at room temperature.

Yield: 20 rolls.

OYSTER STEW

In many homes Christmas Eve would not be complete without a steaming bowl of oyster stew.

4 tablespoons butter
1 tablespoon all-purpose flour
2 cups half-and-half
½ cup milk
1 quart shucked oysters with their liquid
1 tablespoon Worcestershire Sauce
Salt
Freshly ground black pepper
2 tablespoons parsley, finely chopped

Melt the butter in a heavy saucepan. Stir in the flour and cook, stirring, for about 3 minutes to make a roux. Gradually stir in the half-and-half and the milk. Heat through and add the oysters, Worcestershire Sauce, salt, and freshly ground black pepper to taste. Cook over low heat for about 10 minutes until heated through and the edges of the oysters begin to curl. Do not boil. Garnish with parsley and serve hot with crackers.

Yield: 4 to 6 servings.

The whole Christmas thing started in a fine spirit. It was to give happiness to the young, and another holiday to the old, so it was relished by practically everybody. It was a great day, the presents were inexpensive and received with much joy and gratification. . . . The merest little toy was a boon to their young lives, and what a kick it was to the parents to have them rush back up to the bedroom to show you "what Santa brought."

—The Autobiography of Will Rogers

ROAST TURKEY

12- to 14-pound turkey
Salt
Freshly ground black pepper
1 stick unsalted butter, melted
½ cup dry sherry

Preheat oven to 450°F.

Wash the turkey inside and out and dry thoroughly with paper towels. Sprinkle inside cavity with salt and freshly ground black pepper and fill with stuffing. Sew or skewer the cavity shut and truss the turkey.

Place breast side up in a roasting pan and brush with melted butter. Place turkey in oven and reduce temperature to 375°F.

Mix melted butter with the sherry and keep warm. Baste turkey every 30 minutes with the warm sherry-butter. Roast turkey for 3½ to 4 hours, until thermometer inserted into inner thigh registers 180°F. If the breast starts to turn too brown, cover with aluminum foil. Remove foil for last 20 minutes. Remove turkey from oven and let rest for 30 minutes before carving.

Yield: 10 to 12 servings with some leftovers.

CORN BREAD STUFFING

1 day-old corn bread (see following recipe, or use your own)
2 cups white-bread cubes, toasted
2 sticks butter
1 medium onion, finely chopped
3 stalks celery with leaves, finely chopped
1 bunch scallions, trimmed and chopped, green part included
Liver from turkey
1 cup toasted pecans, coarsely chopped (optional, but nice)
½ cup parsley, finely chopped
2 teaspoons salt
½ teaspoon dried thyme
¼ teaspoon cayenne pepper
Freshly ground black pepper
2 eggs, lightly beaten
½ cup Turkey Giblet Stock (see p. 160)

In a large bowl, crumble the corn bread and toss together with the toasted white bread cubes.

In a large skillet, melt 1 stick of butter. Sauté the onion, celery, and scallions in the butter for 15 minutes, until wilted. Do not brown. Add the turkey liver for the last 5 minutes and sauté until brown on the outside but still pink inside. Remove the liver and chop it into small pieces.

Add pecans, parsley, salt, thyme, cayenne, and freshly ground black pepper to taste to the corn bread mixture. Stir in sautéed vegetables and the eggs. Melt remaining stick of butter in the turkey giblet stock. Add turkey giblet stock and melted butter to thoroughly moisten the stuffing. Mix well.

If there is stuffing left over after filling the turkey, put in a buttered casserole, dot with butter on top (optional), cover with foil, and bake for 30 minutes along with the turkey.

Yield: enough stuffing for one 15-pound turkey.

Christmas with Lewis and Clark

Tuesday, 25th December 1804

We were awakened before day by a discharge of three platoons from the party. We had told the Indians not to visit us as it was one of our great medicine days, so that the men remained at home and amused themselves various ways, particularly with dancing, in which they take great pleasure. The American flag was hoisted for the first time in the fort; the best provisions we had were brought out, and this, with a little brandy, enabled them to pass the day in great festivity.

Wednesday, 25th December 1805

We were awakened at daylight by a discharge of firearms, which was followed by a song from the men, as a compliment to us on the return of Christmas, which we have always been accustomed to observe as a day of rejoicing. After breakfast we divided our remaining stock of tobacco, which amounted to twelve carrots, into two parts; one of which we distributed among such of the party as made use of it; making a present of a handkerchief to the others. The remainder of the day was passed in good spirits, though there was nothing in our situation to excite much gayety.

Journals of Meriwether Lewis and William Clark

TURKEY GIBLET STOCK

Make this the day before if possible.

Turkey giblets, but not the liver
Turkey neck
1 small onion, coarsely chopped
1 celery stalk, coarsely chopped
1 carrot, scrubbed and chopped
Handful of parsley with stems
1 teaspoon salt
1/4 teaspoon dried thyme

In a saucepan combine all the above ingredients, together with 4 cups water, and bring to a boil. Reduce heat to low and simmer for 1½ to 2 hours. Strain and refrigerate if keeping overnight. Save the cooked heart and gizzards for gravy if you wish.

Yield: about 2½ cups stock.

GIBLET GRAVY

About 2 cups turkey giblet stock (use all stock not used in stuffing)
2 tablespoons butter, at room temperature
1 tablespoons all-purpose flour
Cooked turkey heart and gizzard, finely chopped
Dash of Tabasco
Salt
Freshly ground black pepper

Pour off most of the fat from the roasting pan. Heat the giblet stock and pour it into the roasting pan and bring to a boil on top of the stove, scraping all the browned bits from the bottom of the pan. Remove from heat. Mash butter and flour together and whisk into the liquid in roasting pan. Set over medium heat and simmer for 5 minutes, stirring constantly. Stir in chopped gizzards and season with Tabasco, salt, and freshly ground black pepper to taste. Pour into gravy boat and serve.

Yield: about 2 cups giblet gravy.

SKILLET CORN BREAD

Corn bread for stuffing should be made at least one day before using. Two days is even better. Leave the bread out, uncovered, to dry out, then crumble it into very small pieces.

2 tablespoons butter or vegetable oil
1½ cups buttermilk
2 large eggs
1 teaspoon salt
1 teaspoon baking powder
½ teaspoon baking soda
2 cups yellow cornmeal, preferably stone-ground

Preheat oven to 450°F.

Place the butter or vegetable oil in a heavy cast-iron 10-inch skillet and put it in the oven to heat while you mix together the corn-bread batter (about 10 minutes).

In a large mixing bowl, whisk together the buttermilk and eggs. Stir in salt, baking powder and baking soda. Stir in the cornmeal to make a batter. Swirl the oil or melted butter to coat the sides of the skillet. Pour the batter into the hot skillet and shake the skillet to smooth the batter. Bake for 20 minutes until it turns a golden brown and edges recede from the sides of the pan.

Yield: 1 corn bread.

Now Christmas comes, 'tis fit that we
Should feast and sing, and merry be:
Keep open house, let fiddlers play,
A fig for cold, sing care away. . . .

Virginia Almanack, 1766

CRANBERRY SAUCE

1 cup water
½ cup orange juice
1 cup sugar
2 cups cranberries, picked over and cleaned

Combine water, orange juice, and sugar in a saucepan. Bring to a boil and cook, stirring until all the sugar is dissolved. Add the cranberries and cook, stirring for 10 to 15 minutes, until cranberries have split and the sauce has thickened a little. Let cool and refrigerate overnight.

Yield: 2 cups cranberry sauce.

JOHN FORD'S GRANDMOTHER'S EGGNOG

This is without a doubt the best eggnog that I have ever tasted. Make it a day ahead because it must stand 24 hours before serving.

6 eggs
1½ to 2 cups sugar
1 quart bourbon whiskey
1 cup rum
1 quart milk
1 quart light cream or half-and-half
Freshly grated nutmeg to taste
1 pint heavy cream

In a large bowl beat the eggs and gradually beat in the sugar until mixture is very light and fluffy. Gradually stir in the bourbon and continue stirring constantly while you add the rum. Stir in milk and light cream or half-and-half. Add grated nutmeg to taste. In a separate bowl beat the heavy cream until stiff and fold it into the eggnog mixture. Cover and refrigerate for 24 hours before serving.

Yield: 20 to 30 servings.

Christmas in the days of my childhood was not the occasion for the orgy of spending and sophisticated entertainment that it now is. Santa Claus was to me neither a very real person nor a dominant myth. He was supposed to have had a hand in fashioning the renewed wardrobe of Annette, the only doll I ever owned, a mature and haughty creature with china head and elaborate chignon. But there was a certain familiarity about the fabrics from which her garments were made that was reminiscent of my mother's piece bag, a fact quite logically arousing some childish doubt.

An orange in the toe of the stocking, a well-polished apple oddly resembling those in our own cellar, a stick or two of pep'mint, cin'mon, or horehound candy, constituted the contents of the average stocking, and quite satisfying they were, too, to a generation of children not sated with useless, destructible, and often soul-destroying junk as are ours today.

Christmas Day was lifted, in our home, only a few degrees above the plane of any other simple holiday.

The Country Kitchen,
Della T. Lutes, 1937

GENIE'S KENTUCKY BOURBON CAKE

This traditional cake is justifiably famous all over America. Rich with pecans, raisins, and Kentucky bourbon whiskey, it is the perfect cake to serve during the Christmas holidays and makes a very special and welcome gift.

The recipe comes from Genie Chipps Henderson, a talented cook and writer. It has been in the Chipps family for generations.

2 teaspoons freshly grated nutmeg
½ cup Kentucky bourbon whiskey
1 pound shelled pecans
½ pound seedless raisins
1½ cups sifted all-purpose flour
1 teaspoon baking powder
½ cup unsalted butter
1 cup sugar
3 egg yolks
3 egg whites, at room temeperature
Pecan halves and candied cherries for decorating cake

Grease a 10-inch tube pan with butter or vegetable shortening and line it with baking parchment. Cut out a circle of baking parchment large enough to cover the top of the pan and reserve it.

Add the nutmeg to the whiskey and let stand while you prepare the rest of the cake ingredients.

Break the pecans in pieces or chop them coarsely. Cut the raisins in half and put them in a bowl with the pecans. Take ½ cup of the sifted flour and mix with the pecans and raisins. This prevents them from sinking to the bottom of the cake when it bakes.

Sift the remaining flour together with the baking powder.

Cream the butter and sugar together until light and fluffy. Beat in the egg yolks, one at a time, until mixture is smooth and pale lemon color. Blend in some of the whiskey, alternating with the flour, until all the whiskey and flour are incorporated into the batter. Fold in pecans and raisins.

Beat the egg whites until they form stiff peaks and fold into the batter. Pour the batter into the prepared cake pan and let stand for 15 minutes while you preheat the oven to 325°F. This allows the batter to settle into the cake pan. Decorate the top of the cake with pecan halves and candied cherries.

Bake at 325°F. for 1 hour and 15 minutes but check to see if the top is browning too quickly. Cover with parchment circle if necessary. After 1 hour and 15 minutes test by pressing the top of the cake with your finger to see if it is firm. If the indentation does not show, the cake is done. Use a cake tester if you like, but remember that the cake should remain slightly moist on the inside. Let it rest for 30 minutes in the cake pan. Remove the cake by placing a plate that is slightly larger than the cake pan over the top and quickly turning the pan upside down. Use another plate to turn the cake over, decorated side up. Cool on a rack and remove the parchment paper. Store the cake in an airtight tin or plastic box.

Yield: one 10-inch cake.

Kentucky Bourbon Balls

These make a fine Christmas confection. It is traditional to make them with dried-out left-over pound cake. Fresh cake will be too moist. If you do not have stale cake, substitute vanilla wafers.

1 cup stale cake crumbs or crushed vanilla wafers
1 cup ground pecans
2 tablespoons light corn syrup
¼ cup good bourbon whiskey
Confectioners' sugar

In a bowl, mix the cake crumbs or crushed vanilla wafers with the ground pecans. Add the cocoa, corn syrup, and bourbon whiskey and mix well until the mixture just holds together. You can knead it slightly with your hands. Take a teaspoonful of dough at a time and mold into balls. Roll the balls in confectioners' sugar and place on an ungreased cookie sheet for several hours to dry. Roll in confectioners' sugar once more and store in a box with a tight-fitting lid. Separate the layers with a sheet of waxed paper. Store these in the refrigerator.

Yield: about 20 bourbon balls.

Hot Spiced Cider

You should never be without the making of this yummy drink to offer to children and teetotalers. It also makes a very soothing nightcap.

1 gallon apple cider
2 cinnamon sticks
3 whole allspice berries

Heat the cider, cinnamon, and allspice in a large saucepan but do not let it boil. Serve hot in large mugs.

Mulled Cider

This version is definitely not for the teetotaler, but it is very satisfying to a throat made sore from too much caroling, and the body made weary from too much festivity.

1 gallon apple cider
12 whole cloves
12 whole allspice
6 sticks cinnamon
1 cup brown sugar
1 bottle Calvados or applejack

Pour the cider into a large saucepan. Tie the cloves, allspice, and cinnamon into a piece of cheesecloth and add to the cider. Add the brown sugar. Heat gently to a simmer and stir until the sugar is completely dissolved. Simmer very gently for about 10 minutes to blend the flavors. Pour in the Calvados or applejack and heat until hot but not boiling. Serve in large mugs.

Yield: about 24 servings.

HOT MULLED WINE

2 cups water
1 cinnamon stick
6 whole cloves
½ teaspoon grated nutmeg
Peel of 1 lemon, finely sliced
½ cup sugar
1 cup cognac
2 bottles red Burgundy wine

Place the water, cinnamon stick, cloves, nutmeg, and lemon peel into a saucepan and simmer for 30 minutes. Strain the water and return to the saucepan. Add the sugar and heat, stirring until the sugar is completely dissolved. Add the cognac and wine. Cook gently until just hot, but do not boil. Serve hot.

Yield: about 12 servings.

HOT BUTTERED RUM

2 quarts water
1½ cups brown sugar
1 stick unsalted butter
4 sticks cinnamon
6 whole cloves
1 whole nutmeg
1 bottle dark rum

In a large enameled kettle place the water, sugar, butter, cinnamon, cloves, and nutmeg. Simmer gently for 2 hours. Add the rum, heat through but do not boil, and serve.

Yield: 12 to 16 servings.

Christmas with the Shakers

At seven-thirty P.M. on Christams Eve a bell sounded and all the Shakers retired to their quarters. One of their number in each building read the story of the washing of the disciples' feet from the Book of John. They then washed each other's feet. The members of the singing groups then departed surreptitiously to a shop some distance from the dwelling house for a final practice. By prior arrangement with the elder in charge of the shop, a fire had been built and the singers were admitted to the shop upon giving a secret signal. The final rehearsal was completed before nine o'clock. The singers departed and the village was cloaked in silence.

At four-thirty on Christmas morning, the singers awoke, hurried to the kitchen for a light repast, and then set out for the family dwellings in horse-drawn sleighs. At each building they sang their specially prepared Christmas songs and hastened on to each house where members of the three North Union families lived. Their rounds completed, the singers and all other members of the colony gathered at the sisters' dwelling houses at ten A.M. for a union meeting. The men and boys sat on one side and the women and girls on the other side of the room. They reminisced together of Christmases past, sang religious songs, and ate nuts and popcorn. At eleven o'clock a light lunch was brought to the sisters' dwelling houses. After lunch all of the members went to the meeting house, which stood at the northeast corner of the present-day intersection of Lee Road and Shaker Boulevard. There, a service similar to the usual Sunday church program was held. In addition, special Christmas hymns were sung and there was reading from the Scriptures. At the conclusion of the church service the barrel of selected apples was opened and the contents distributed, along with special gifts which had been carefully made.

Then came the great feast when the finest delicacies of the Shaker kitchens were spread upon the holiday festive board. When the meal was finished a big basket was passed around the room and each person placed an offering of clothing or some other useful gift in it for the poor people. These gifts were then distributed to needy persons in Cleveland or on nearby farms. The day closed with singing and the Shakers once again ready to "put their hands to work and their hearts to God."

The Shaker Historical Society,
Shaker Heights, Ohio

Figgy Pudding

This rich fruitcake will satisfy the most demanding guests and carolers who stop by during the Christmas season.

1 cup figs, roughly chopped
1 cup dark seedless raisins
1 cup currants
½ cup candied orange peel, thinly sliced
½ cup walnuts, coarsely chopped
2½ cups flour
½ teaspoon baking soda
2 teaspoons baking powder
1 teaspoon cinnamon
½ teaspoon nutmeg
½ teaspoon mace
½ teaspoon salt
1 stick unsalted butter, at room temperature
½ cup brown sugar
½ cup maple syrup
2 eggs
1 cup buttermilk
¼ cup Cointreau or other orange-flavored liqueur

Preheat oven to 350°F. Grease a 9-inch tube pan with butter or solid vegetable shortening and line with baking parchment.

Mix the figs, raisins, currants, candied orange peel, and walnuts together in a bowl. Add ½ cup of the flour and toss to mix well. Make sure that each piece of fruit and nut is well dusted with flour, as this will keep the pieces from sinking to the bottom of the pudding.

Sift together the remaining flour, baking soda, baking powder, cinnamon, nutmeg, mace, and salt.

Cream butter and sugar together until light and fluffy. Beat in the maple syrup and the eggs, one at a time, beating until the mixture is frothy and pale-colored. Beat in the buttermilk and Cointreau or other orange-flavored liqueur. Stir the flour and spices into the liquid ingredients and mix well. Fold in the fruits and nuts. Spoon the mixture into the prepared 9-inch tube pan. Bake for 1 hour or until a cake tester inserted into the center comes out dry.

Serve warm with Brandy Hard Sauce (following recipe).

Yield: 8 to 10 servings.

Now bring us some figgy pudding,
Now bring us some figgy pudding,
Now bring us some figgy pudding,
And bring it out here.

We won't go until we get some,
We won't go until we get some,
We won't go until we get some,
So bring it out here.

We all love figgy pudding,
We all love figgy pudding,
We all love figgy pudding,
So bring some out here.

We wish you a Merry Christmas,
We wish you a Merry Christmas,
We wish you a Merry Christmas,
And a Happy New Year!

Old English or Scottish song

BRANDY HARD SAUCE

1 cup (2 sticks) unsalted butter, at room temperature
1¾ cups confectioners' sugar
Brandy or cognac, as needed

Cream butter and sugar together to make a stiff paste. Beat in brandy or cognac gradually to add as much as the mixture can absorb and still remain on the stiff side. Place in a pretty serving dish and refrigerate before serving.

Yield: about 1 cup sauce.

WHITE FRUITCAKE

This is a traditional Christmas cake in many parts of the country, particularly the South.

1 pound white raisins
1½ cups candied pineapple, diced
1½ cups dried apricots, coarsely chopped

½ cup candied orange peel, finely sliced
2 cups blanched almonds, coarsely chopped
1½ cups pecans, coarsely chopped
½ cup walnuts, coarsely chopped
4 cups sifted all-purpose flour
1 teaspoon baking powder
½ teaspoon salt
1½ teaspoons cinnamon
1 teaspoon allspice
1 teaspoon nutmeg
1 cup unsalted butter
2 cups sugar
6 large eggs
½ cup dry sherry
1 teaspoon vanilla

Preheat oven to 350°F.

Grease two 4-by-8½-inch loaf pans with butter or vegetable shortening. Line the bottom with baking parchment.

In a large bowl mix together the raisins, pineapple, apricots, orange peel, almonds, and walnuts. Add ½ cup of flour and mix well to make sure all the fruit and nuts are well covered with flour.

Sift remaining 3½ cups flour together with the baking powder, salt, cinnamon, allspice, and nutmeg.

Cream together the sugar and butter until light and fluffy. Beat in the eggs one at a time. Beat in the sherry and vanilla.

Stir the fruits and nuts into the egg mixture, then stir in flour and spices to make a smooth batter. Spoon the batter into the prepared pans and smooth the tops with spoon or spatula.

Bake at 350°F. for 1 hour. Check to see that the top is not browning too quickly. If necessary, cover with baking parchment. After 1 hour, press the top lightly with your fingers; if the cake springs back into shape, it is done.

Let cool in pans for 30 minutes. Remove from pans and carefully peel away the baking parchment. Cool completely on wire racks. Brush cakes with brandy or whiskey and wrap tightly. Store tightly covered in a cool place.

Yield: Two 4-by-8½-inch cakes

Alphabetical Index of Recipes

Recipe Index by Category

OTHER MAIN DISHES

RITUAL FOODS

SALADS

SAUCES

SIDE DISHES

SOUPS

SWEETS